24 June 22

KATHLEEN
HALE
IS A
CRAZY
STALKER

Also by Kathleen Hale

No One Else Can Have You

Nothing Bad Is Going to Happen

KATHLEEN HALE IS A CRAZY STALKER

SIX ESSAYS

Kathleen Hale

Grove Press

New York

The pieces in this collection were all previously published and have been updated and edited for this book publication. Names were changed, including in original publications, to protect identities.

FIRST EDITION

Published simultaneously in Canada
Printed in the United States of America

This title was set in 11 point Berling LT
by Alpha Design & Composition of Pittsfield, NH

First Grove Atlantic hardcover edition: June 2019

Library of Congress Cataloging-in-Publication data is available for this title.

ISBN 978-0-8021-2909-3
eISBN 978-0-8021-4691-5

Grove Press
an imprint of Grove Atlantic
154 West 14th Street
New York, NY 10011

Distributed by Publishers Group West

groveatlantic.com

19 20 21 22   10 9 8 7 6 5 4 3 2 1

For my daughter.

May your mistakes feel like adventures.

Contents

KATHLEEN
HALE
IS A
CRAZY
STALKER

Catfish

In the months before my first novel came out, I was a charmless lunatic—the type that other lunatics cross the street to avoid. I fidgeted and talked to myself, rewriting out loud passages of a book that had already gone to print. I remember when my editor handed me the final copy: I held the book in my hands for a second before grabbing a pen and scribbling edits in the margins.

"No," she said firmly, taking the pen away. "Kathleen, you understand we can't make any more changes, right?"

"I was JK," I lied.

Anxious and inexperienced, I began checking Goodreads, a social reviewing site now owned by Amazon. My publisher, HarperTeen, had sent advance copies of my young adult novel to bloggers and I wanted to see what they thought. Other authors warned me not to do this, but I didn't listen. Soon, my daily visits tallied somewhere between "slightly more than is attractive to admit here" and infinity.

For the most part, I found Goodreaders were awarding my novel one star or five stars, with nothing in between. "Well, it's a weird book," I reminded myself. "It's about a girl with PTSD teaming up with a veteran to solve her best friend's grisly murder." Mostly I was relieved they weren't *all* one-star reviews.

3

Prior to my book deal I wasn't on social media. Picking a photo or something to say in front of everyone made me nervous. But my editors urged me to build a "web presence." There would be no book tour, no launch events, they explained. In lieu of a publicity budget, I'd gain access to an in-house social media team that consisted of two recent college graduates, who by virtue of their youth made everyone else look like dinosaurs and had been trusted to make things "go viral." No one had yet determined the actual relationship between tweets and blog posts and book sales.* But we were willing to bet that likes and followers led to popularity or even a small brand of celebrity, which could be leveraged, we hoped—someday, somehow—for money.

As my publication date loomed in the distance, the two young women on this media team encouraged me to tweet every day, to interact with every reader who tweeted at me, and to accept every interview request, even if it was from a blogger who had thirty-eight followers and described herself, in her official bio, as "loves to reed ☺." I was enlisted to host the media team at my house for several hours so they could make a video of me standing in various places, to write long posts that no one read about what it was like to write my

---

* I'd later find out from an inside source at HarperCollins that if you tweet a link to your book, probably less than 5 percent of your followers will click on it, and even fewer will buy it as a result.

book, and to do "giveaways" of signed books and other items that I'd paid for with my own money. The time and cash I spent trying to "promote my brand" cut into my actual writing schedule. But I'd been taught to think that public relations was part of my job as a modern writer, an otherwise solitary profession that had in no way prepared me to interact with other human beings, period, much less "network" with them. I don't know how to talk to people—that's why I write. But I was the dinosaur, a naïve one. I walked into the spotlight expecting applause.

One night, while deleting and rewriting the same tweet over and over, a tiny avatar popped up on my screen. She was young, tanned, and beautiful, with dark hair and a bright smile. Her Twitter profile said she was a book blogger, tenth grade teacher, wife, and mother of two. From what I could tell she tweeted nonstop between six p.m. and midnight, usually about the TV show *Gossip Girl.* According to her bio, her name was Blythe Harris, and she'd written saying she had some ideas for my next book.

"Cool, Blythe, thanks!" I replied. In an attempt to connect with readers, I'd been asking Twitter for ideas—"The weirdest thing you can think of!"—promising to try to incorporate them in the sequel.

Eager to see if Blythe had read my book, I clicked through the daisy chain of her social media, from her Twitter to her blog to her Goodreads page, where I saw she had given my young adult novel a one-star rating. "Meh," I thought. I scrolled down her review.

"Fuck this," it said. "I think this book is awfully written and offensive; its execution in regards to all aspects is horrible and honestly, nonexistent." Blythe went on to warn other readers that I was a rape apologist and slut shamer. She said my book mocked everything from domestic abuse to PTSD. She'd only read the first chapter, she explained, but wished Goodreads allowed users to leave scores of zero, because that's what my novel deserved. "I can say with utmost certainty that this is one of the worst books I've read this year," she said, "maybe my life."

Other commenters joined the thread to say they'd been thinking of reading my book, but now wouldn't. Or they said that they'd liked it, but could see where Blythe was coming from and would reduce their ratings.

"Rape is brushed off as if it is nothing," Blythe explained to one commenter. "PTSD is referred to insensitively; domestic abuse is the punch line of a joke, as is mental illness."

I shook my head, wondering how I could possibly be guilty of mocking mental illness, when I had it myself, and of all that bad rape stuff Blythe accused me of, when I'd been raped myself.

"There isn't rape in my book," I told my fiancé.

"Why did you wake me up to tell me that?" he asked.

I went back to my pillow and racked my brain, trying to see again where I had gone wrong. I wished I could magically transform all the copies being printed with a quick swish of my little red pen. "Not to make fun of my own PTSD or anything, because that would be wrong," I might add to one character's comment.

At the bottom of the page, Goodreads had issued the following directive (if you were signed in as an author, it appeared after every bad review of a book you'd written): "We really, really (really!) don't think you should comment on this review, even to thank the reviewer. If you think this review is against our Review Guidelines, please flag it to bring it to our attention. Keep in mind that if this is a review of the book, even one including factual errors, we generally will not remove it.

"If you still feel you must leave a comment, click 'Accept and Continue' below to proceed (but again, we don't recommend it)."

I would soon learn why.

*　　*　　*

After listening to me yammer on about the Goodreads review, my well-meaning mother sent me a link to a website called Stop The Goodreads Bullies. ("I don't think you're allowed to call it bullying unless kids are involved," I said. But she encouraged me to check it out.) Blythe appeared on a page called

Badly Behaving Goodreaders, an allusion to the term Badly Behaving Authors—or "BBA," a popular acronym employed by Goodreaders to describe authors they didn't like. (In the comment thread under Blythe's review, "BBA" appeared several times.) When I emailed the cofounder of STGRB, Athena Parker, she told me that BBAs are "usually authors who [have] unknowingly broken some 'rule.'" In my case, I'd become a BBA by writing a book containing "triggering" materials. Other authors had earned the title for tweeting their dislike of snarky reviews, or supporting other BBAs. Parker warned that once an author was labeled a BBA, the entire book-blogging community unofficially blacklisted his or her book. She also told me to stay far away from Blythe Harris. "Blythe was involved in an [online] attack on a fourteen-year-old girl back in May 2012," Parker said. Apparently the teenager had written a glowing review of a book Blythe hated, obliquely referencing Blythe's hatred for it: "Dear Haters," the review read. "Everyone has his or her own personal opinion, but expressing that through profanity is not the answer." (Blythe had cursed in her review.) In response, Blythe rallied her followers, and adults began flooding the girl's thread, saying, among other things, "Fuck you."

It turned out that Parker and her cofounders were not the only ones to have run into trouble with Blythe and her followers. Over time, I would randomly meet a couple other authors who'd been attacked by either her or her followers. One had written a female protagonist into his young adult novel, *Fire-cracker*, and was subsequently hounded by a blogger named Ashlee, who called him a misogynist for even attempting to capture the female experience and wrote a scathing review of his book, the link for which she continued to tweet weekly for years. When his wife (unbeknownst to him) sent Ashlee a harmless email, asking her to please stop, Ashlee published the email on her blog, claiming that she'd been threatened and was now traumatized. An editor friend encouraged me to get in touch with other authors she knew who had been negatively reviewed by Blythe. Only one agreed to talk, under the condition of anonymity. She remained terrified that any more beef with Blythe might ruin her career. Like Parker, she considered Blythe dangerous.

I'll call her Patricia Winston.

"You know Blythe, too?" I Gchatted her.

She responded—"Omg"—and immediately took our con-versation off the record.

"DO NOT ENGAGE," she implored me. "You'll make yourself look bad, and she'll ruin you."

* * *

Writing for a living means working in an industry where one's success or failure hinges on the subjective reactions of an audience. But, as Patricia implied, caring too much looks narcissistic. A stand-up comic can deal with a heckler in a crowded theater, but online etiquette prohibits writers from responding to negativity in any way.

In the following weeks, Blythe's vitriol continued to create a ripple effect: every time someone admitted to having liked my book on Twitter or Goodreads, they included a caveat that referenced her review. The ones who truly loathed it tweeted reviews at me. It got to the point where my mild-mannered mother (also checking on my book's status) wanted to run a background check on Blythe. "Who are these people?" she asked. Then she accidentally followed Blythe on Twitter—"I didn't know the button!" she yelled over the phone—and started getting cyberbullied herself, by Blythe's small but fanatical army. ("Fine, I'll get off the Twitter," she said. "But I really don't like these people.")

That same day, Blythe began tweeting in tandem with me, ridiculing everything I said. Confronting her would mean publicly acknowledging that I searched my name on Twitter, which is about as socially attractive as setting up a Google alert for your name (which I also did). So instead I ate a lot of candy and engaged in light stalking: I prowled Blythe's Instagram and Twitter, read her reviews, considered photos of her elaborate baked goods, and watched from a distance as she got on her soapbox—at one point bragging she was the only person she knew who used her real name and profession online. As my fascination mounted, and my self-loathing deepened, I reminded myself that there were worse things than rabid bloggers (cancer, for instance) and that people suffered greater degradations than becoming writers. But still, I wanted to respond.

Patricia warned me that this was exactly what Blythe was waiting for—and Athena Parker agreed: "[GR Bullies] actually bait authors online to get them to say something, anything, that can be taken out of context." The next step, she said, was for them to begin the "career-destroying" phase.

"Is this even real?" I Gchatted Patricia.

"YES THERE IS A CAREER-DESTROYING PHASE. IT'S AWFUL. DO. NOT. ENGAGE. Omg did you put our convo back on the record?"

She went invisible.

I sighed, feeling lonely, and switched from Gmail to Google Scholar. Recent studies had dark things to say about abusive internet commenters—a University of Manitoba report suggested they shared traits with child molesters and serial killers. The more I wondered about Blythe, the more I was reminded of something Sarah Silverman said in an article for *Entertainment Weekly*: "A guy once just yelled, 'ME!!' in the middle of my set. It was amazing. This guy's heckle actually directly equaled its heartbreaking subtext—'me!!'" Silverman, an avid fan of

Howard Stern, went on to describe a poignant moment she remembered from listening to his radio show: Stern was about to hang up on an asshole caller, when the caller blurted out, in a crazed, stuttering voice, "I exist!" I had a feeling the motivation behind heckling, or trolling, was similar to why most people do anything—why I write, for instance, or why I was starting to treat typing my name into search boxes like it was a job. Despite our differences it occurred to me Blythe and I had this much in common: we were both obsessed with being seen.

I wanted to talk to Blythe—to convince her I was a real person with real feelings and that my book was really good—and my self-control was dwindling. One afternoon, good-naturedly drunk on bourbon and after watching Blythe tweet about her in-progress manuscript, I subtweeted that, while weird, derivative reviews could be irritating, it was a relief to remember that all bloggers were also aspiring authors.

My notifications feed exploded. Bloggers who'd been nice to me were hurt. Those who already hated me now had an excuse to write long posts about what a bitch I was, making it clear that:

1) Reviews are for readers, not authors.
2) When authors engage with reviewers, it's abusive behavior.

"Sorry," I pleaded on Twitter. "Didn't mean *all* bloggers, just the ones who talk shit then tweet about their in-progress manuscripts." I responded a few more times, digging myself deeper. For the rest of the afternoon, I tried to neutralize venom from teenagers and grown women alike. A few people stood up for me and were immediately attacked. So they deleted any mention of me, or switched sides and joined the hubbub to survive.

Eventually I emailed an apology to a blogger who still liked me. After she posted it, people quieted on Twitter, and my inbox quit sagging with unread mail. But the one-star reviews continued, and this time they all called me a BBA. The career-destroying phase had begun, and I longed to meet with its commander and broker a peace treaty. I imagined myself sitting down with Blythe for drinks. Sure, there would be an initial moment of awkward silence. But then we would cry and admit to a deep-seated, mutual admiration, realizing with delight that underneath our acrimony had been a friendship waiting to happen. Then we would feast on her elaborate baked goods and laugh and laugh and laugh.

Just then, out of the corner of my eye, I noticed a discrepancy in Blythe's social media profiles; in one, she said she was an eighth grade teacher, but another said tenth grade. This didn't seem all that strange to me—some of my teacher friends go from grade to grade—but in my eagerness to demystify this woman, I wanted to know the exact details of everything she did. So I typed her name into the internet.

Although I'd read all the reviews she'd ever written on Goodreads, I had somehow never googled her, which was odd, given how many things I googled every single day. (One recent search inquired, "mcdonalds stop make pizza 90s why?") But when I googled Blythe Harris, there was nothing to be found—which was weird, considering she was a high school staff member. It suddenly dawned on me that Blythe probably wasn't her real name. So I dug a little deeper. I noticed she tweeted and uploaded blog posts during school hours. Admittedly, a lot of people I knew went on social media at work, but my teacher friends didn't—they just didn't have time. So was she maybe not a teacher, either?

I clicked back to Blythe's Instagram, scrolling through the hundreds of now-familiar photos, and realized, for the first time, that none of them included human beings. Other than her main profile picture, which was the same on every site, she posted pictures only of her baked goods, her home's majestic interiors, a Pomeranian, and the packages of books she received from publishers like mine.

I reminded myself that some people were private. Hence the presumably fake name. Also, just because "Blythe" was perfect looking didn't mean she had to post selfies. She had other things to do, like cook beautiful meals for her adoring family and live in her mansion. I zoomed in on a picture of her entryway, with its marble floor and two-story-tall vaulted ceiling, pretending that I lived there. At the bottom, I noticed a thin white band and partial lettering.

I knew right away what I was seeing—because I'd saved enough of Blythe's tweets to know what a screenshot looked like. The white space and lettering at the bottom of Blythe's photo marked it as stolen. She'd grabbed it from someone's life and had forgotten to crop out the evidence before posting.

So, was anything about this woman real?

The idea that Blythe might be fake made me feel normal for the first time in days. If I could discount her existence, I could discount everything that she had said. If I could prove to myself she was a bogeyman, then I could finally wake up.

I had no ideas for how to fact-check her identity. But the next morning, after several more glasses of bourbon, I had a really bad idea.

* * *

After my book came out, a book blogger emailed me saying she wanted to publish a series of author interviews by bloggers on her site. She'd asked me to participate and had offered to let me pick any blogger I wanted.

I wrote back as fast as I could. My sweaty fingertips slid across the keys: "Blythe Harris. I choose Blythe Harris to interview me."

The book blogger responded saying she'd reach out to Blythe on my behalf. Then she wrote back saying Blythe had agreed to do the interview (I screamed with joy). The book club explained that it was common for authors to do "giveaways" in conjunction with the interview, and asked if I could sign some books. I agreed, and they forwarded me Blythe's address.

The exterior of the house that showed up on Google Maps looked thousands of square feet too small for the interiors Blythe had posted on Instagram. According to the telephone directory and recent census reports, nobody named Blythe Harris lived there. The address belonged to someone I'll call Judy Donofrio, who, according to an internet background check ($19), was forty-six—not twenty-seven, as Blythe was—and was a vice president at a company that authorized disability claims. She lived less than an hour away from me by car.

It looked as if I had been taken in by someone using a fake identity.

I Gchatted Patricia: "I think we've been catfished?"

Patricia asked how I could be sure Judy D. wasn't merely renting to Blythe H.?

I clicked over to the active Gchat I had going with my best friend, Sarah McKetta, one of the smartest people I know, and sent her all the current "evidence" I had. Did McKetta think I was right?

"Well, there's only one way to find out," she said, and sent me a car rental link. "Go talk to her."

Authors and reviewers have a long history of showdowns. Proust famously challenged his worst critic to a duel. Dale Peck, known for his icy and crotchety book reviews, was pied in the face by Rick Moody (he called Moody the worst author of his generation) and slapped (twice!) by author Stanley Crouch. Gore Vidal wrote an essay slamming Norman Mailer, and when the two appeared on *The Dick Cavett Show*, Mailer headbutted Vidal backstage. By comparison my agenda felt tame. All I wanted to do was see Blythe's real face, and maybe talk to it.

"DO NOT DO THIS," Patricia cautioned me, and if only I had listened to her, I might have saved myself a world of trouble.

Instead, I clicked on the link for the rental car.

* * *

I planned my car rental for a few months down the line. I was procrastinating, hoping to untangle the mystery without face-to-face confrontation. I sent a message to Blythe through the book blogger, asking if we could do the interview via video chat. She vanished for a month, then told the blogger she'd been dealing with family issues and didn't see herself having the time to do a video chat. So I asked the blogger to ask Blythe whether we might do the interview via phone, instead, and Blythe countered by pulling out of the interview altogether— she had to go to Europe, she explained, but she hoped I'd still address "the drama," a reference to my drunken tweets.

"Europe" seemed a vague destination for an adult planning a vacation. But a few nights later, lit only by the glow of my screen, I watched in real time as Blythe uploaded photos of Greece to Instagram. The Acropolis at night. An ocean view. A box of macaroons in an anonymous hand. The images looked generic to me, the kind you can easily find on Google Images. But then Blythe posted a picture of herself sitting in a helicopter. The face matched the tanned Twitter photograph. My initial reaction was jealousy, tinged with embarrassment. I was wrong. Blythe was real. And her life was fucking fantastic. But then I clicked over to Facebook, and saw that Judy Donofrio— the owner of Blythe's house—had updated her own profile with photographs of a vacation in Oyster Bay, New York. I clicked through and saw that the holiday had started on the same day as Blythe Harris's.

* * *

In preparation for my surprise visit, I thought it might be helpful to get some expert advice about meeting a catfish in person. So I telephoned Nev Schulman, who was (at the time*) known and celebrated for his 2010 hit documentary *Catfish*, which had first coined the now-mainstream term,** and for hosting and producing the MTV spinoff show, *Catfish*, in which he helped people confront their long-distance internet boyfriends, girlfriends, and enemies—almost 100 percent of whom ended up being fakes. Maybe, I thought, he could help me, too.

"Of all the catfish I've confronted, there was only one I didn't tell I was coming," Nev said cagily, apparently shocked by my plan to go to Blythe's unannounced. Nonetheless, he had some tips: "This is a woman who is used to sitting behind her computer and saying whatever she wants with very little accountability. Even if she hears from people she criticizes, she doesn't have to look them in the face. She doesn't know she hurt your feelings, and she doesn't really care."

---

* Nev's show was later suspended, due to accusations of which he was formally acquitted but nevertheless ended that stage of his career because they went viral on the internet.

** The title reference comes at the very end of the documentary, during an interview with the man whose wife catfished Nev. He tries to explain her behavior with an allusion to the practice of shipping codfish overseas: "By the time the codfish reached China, the flesh was mush and tasteless. So this guy came up with the idea that if you put these cods in these big vats, put some catfish in with them and the catfish will keep the cod agile. And there are those people who are catfish in life. And they keep you on your toes."

For a moment I felt deeply understood, as if I were talking to someone with psychic powers. "How did you know that she hurt my feelings?" I asked.

In a tone like, *duh*, Nev responded, "Because you're going to her house."

He urged me to listen to whoever answered the door and not to make our impromptu meeting about my "issues."

Throughout our conversation Nev used the word "issues" so many times that I decided to speak on the phone with another kind of expert: a doctor. Former filmmaker Dr. Michael Rich splits his time between teaching pediatrics at Harvard Medical School and lecturing on "Society, Human Development and Health" at Harvard's School of Public Health. He is also the director of the Center on Media and Child Health at Boston Children's Hospital and runs a webpage called Ask the Mediatrician, where parents write in about concerns ranging from cyberbullying to catfishing. Given the adolescent nature of my problem, he seemed like he would be an excellent resource.

"The internet doesn't make you crazy," he said. "But you can make yourself crazy on the internet."

I asked Rich about his catfished patients: How did they react in the months that followed their discovery? "Depression, anxiety. They tend to spend more time online rather than less." I glanced at my browser window, currently open to three Blythe Harris platforms. "They're hyper vigilant, always checking their phone. Certainly substance abuse." I swallowed some whiskey. "The response is going to vary," he concluded, "but it will have a commonality of self-loathing and self-harm."

"Great," I said, half listening.

I double-checked Blythe's address.

* * *

I parked down the street from Blythe/Judy's house. It wasn't a mansion but looked like something from a storybook, complete with dormer windows and a lush, colorful garden. It was only now occurring to me that I didn't really know what to say and should probably have brought a present. I needed a white flag.

I searched my bag, but all it contained besides notebooks and tampons was a tiny book I'd been given and hadn't read yet: Anna Quindlen's *A Short Guide to a Happy Life*. This seemed a little passive-aggressive, but I figured it was better than nothing.

Before I could change my mind, I walked briskly down the street toward the Mazda parked in Blythe/Judy's driveway. A hooded sweatshirt with pink lips emblazoned across the chest lay on the passenger seat; in the back was a large folder full of what looked like insurance claims. I heard tires on gravel and turned to see a police van. For a second I thought I was going to be arrested, but it was passing by—just a drive through a quiet neighborhood where the only thing suspicious was me.

I strolled to the front door. A dog barked and I thought of Blythe's Instagram Pomeranian. Was it the same one? The doorbell had been torn off, and up close the garden was overgrown. I started to feel hot and claustrophobic. The stupid happiness book grew sweaty in my hands. I couldn't decide whether to knock.

The curtains were drawn, but I could see a figure silhouetted in one window, looking at me.

The barking stopped.

I dropped the book on the step and ran away.

* * *

Over the course of an admittedly privileged life, I consider my visit to Blythe/Judy's as a sort of personal rock bottom. In the weeks that followed, unable to verify Blythe's real identity in person, I felt certain the conclusion to the Blythe Harris mystery was simply "Kathleen Hale is crazy"—and to be fair, that is one deduction. But I soon found out that it was not the only one, because while pondering that version of this story, I continued to scroll through both Blythe's and Judy's social media pages. And that's when I saw something I had missed: Blythe had recently posted photos of the same dogs from

Judy's Facebook page, even using their names—Bentley and Bailey—but saying they were hers.

I sent screenshots to Patricia, expecting her usual incredulity. But instead of debating me, she told me I was right—we'd been catfished—the dogs were the missing puzzle piece.

"It's the end of an era," she Gchatted me.

Between the emoticons and the lowercase font, she was the calmest version of herself I'd ever seen.

"This is closure," she said. "I am at peace now."

But I couldn't say the same for myself. I wasn't satisfied and still yearned for some kind of interaction. To me, closure meant hearing Judy admit to being Blythe—not necessarily to the world, but to me. Instead of returning to Judy's house and knocking on her door, which still felt like the biggest breach of decency I'd ever pulled, I decided to call her at work. McKetta and I rehearsed the conversation.

"What do I even say?" I kept asking.

"Just pretend to be a fact-checker," she said.

"So now I'm catfishing her?"

"Big time," McKetta said.

* * *

I called the number, expecting to get sent to an operator. But a human answered, and when I asked for Judy, she put me through.

"This is Judy Donofrio," she said.

I spat out the line about needing to fact-check a piece. She seemed uncertain but agreed to answer some questions.

"Is this how to spell your name?" I asked, and spelled it.

"Next question," she snapped without answering.

"Do you live in Nassau County?"

"No." she said. Judy's Facebook page and LinkedIn account said otherwise, and that's where her house supposedly was. She was lying, in other words, but I didn't push it.

I asked if she was a vice president at her company.

"I can't help you," she said. "Buh-bye . . ."

"DO YOU USE THE NAME BLYTHE HARRIS TO BOOK BLOG ONLINE?" I felt like the guy on *The Howard Stern Show*, screaming, "I exist!"

"No," she said quietly.

She paused before adding, "Who's Blythe Harris?"

Her tone had changed, as if suddenly she could talk forever.

"She's a book blogger," I said, "and she's given your address."

"A book blog . . . Yeah, I don't know what that is."

"Oh."

We both mumbled about how weird it all was.

"She uses photos of your dogs," I said, feeling like the biggest creep in the world, but also that I might be talking to a slightly bigger creep. "I have it here," I said, pretending to consult notes, even though she couldn't see me, "that you have a Pomeranian and another dog, and she uses photos that you posted."

She gasped. "I do have a Pomeranian."

"She uses your address," I repeated. "Do you have children who might be using a different name online?" I already knew she had two teenagers.

"Nope—I do, but they're not . . . They don't live there anymore," she stammered. "You know what?" she added. "I am Judy, but I don't know who this Blythe Harris is and why she's using my pictures or information." I could hear her lips smacking; unruffled, she had started snacking. "Can you report her or something?"

"Unfortunately, it's not a crime," I said. "It's called catfishing."

She didn't know what that meant, so I found myself defining "catfishing" for someone who was, presumably, catfishing me (and whom I was cross-catfishing). "It happens a lot."

"A long time ago I used to get books," she said, her mouth full. "I just put 'Return to Sender.'"

I told her that publishing houses were sending the books. I told her she might want to check out Blythe Harris's Instagram, as there were photos on it she would recognize. She didn't seem to care.

I asked how long it had been since she'd last received books.

"Like years ago," she said.

An hour after I got off the phone to Judy, Blythe Harris deleted her Twitter and set her Instagram to private. A contact at a publishing house confirmed that they'd been sending books to Judy's address all year and as recently as two weeks prior, addressed to Blythe.

* * *

"So," I asked Nev Schulman, after giving him my evidence. "Am I a good catfisherwoman?"

"Do you really need me to tell you that?" he asked, sounding tired. He added, "What's interesting are the unanswered questions—like, why would she do this? That's something our show does. It gives people closure. I'm tempted to tell you to call her back and tell her it's you and that you lied to her— because, look, I'm curious to know about this chick, too—these people are really interesting, and the lives they lead and the characters they create, it takes a lot of brain power."

So I called Judy again, and this time I told her that I knew she was Blythe Harris.

She started yelling. She said she wasn't Blythe Harris and that she was going to call the police about "this Blythe Harris person."

I paused. "Okay." I hadn't anticipated the shouting.

"The profile picture is not me," Judy cried, referring to Blythe's Twitter profile. "It's my friend Carla."

I gasped. "You know that person?"

"She stole [pictures of Carla] off my website from making my Facebook."

The way she spoke about the internet—"making my Facebook"—made doubt grow in my chest. Blythe's blog was nothing fancy, but it had obviously been generated by someone who knew her way around a basic html template.

"The Pomeranian is me," Judy said. "That picture isn't me."

She wouldn't give me Carla's last name, but I later found her by searching Judy's Facebook friends. Sure enough, Blythe Harris had dragged her Twitter profile picture from Carla's Facebook. The only picture on Blythe's Instagram page that featured an actual person—the one of the woman in the helicopter—had also been repurposed from a Facebook album chronicling Carla's recent trip to Greece.

I asked Judy if she had told Carla about Blythe Harris. She hadn't: "I don't want to alarm her." Then she started yelling again.

"I'm not yelling at you," she yelled, and started to cry.

"I'm sorry," I said.

"I feel like this is my fault," Judy sobbed.

"How is it your fault?" I wanted to know.

"Whatever," she whispered darkly. "People are stupid. If you track their IP address, you can find them easily."

This seemed at odds with her earlier Facebook naïveté, but I felt too suffocated to parse it all out. "Okay," I said. "Feel better." When I gave her my name and number, there was no obvious reaction to my identity. "If you discover anything," I said, "or if there's anything you feel like you forgot to say, please let me know." Sweat trickled down my back. I knew, on some level, that I was speaking to the person behind Blythe Harris. But after all this time, and all this digging, I still couldn't conclusively prove it. Part of me wondered whether it even mattered anymore.

"Sure," she said. "I'll Facebook message you."

After we hung up, she blocked me on Facebook. Then Blythe Harris reconnected her Twitter account and set it to private. But she was still following me, which meant I could send her a direct message. I wrote to her that I knew she was using other women's photos. I filled up three of the 140-character word limits, imploring her to contact me.

"I'm not trying to embarrass you," I wrote. Channeling Schulman, I emphasized that I just wanted to know more about her experience—to listen and hear how she felt about all this. Blythe responded by unfollowing me; there could be no more direct messages.

I'm told Blythe still blogs and posts on Goodreads; Patricia tells me she still live tweets *Gossip Girl*. In some ways I'm grateful that her Twitter and Instagram are set to private, because it has helped me drop that obsessive part of my daily routine. Although, like anyone with a tendency toward low-grade insanity, I occasionally grow nostalgic for the thing that made me nuts.

Unlike iPhone or Facebook messages, Twitter doesn't confirm receipt of direct messages. Even so, I return now and then to our one-way conversation, wanting so badly for the time stamp at the bottom of my message to read "Seen."

* * *

Months later, after I published a version of this essay in the *Guardian*, Dr. Rich's warning proved true, and I went bananas. I lost my mind.

Admittedly, I'd never had the sturdiest of dispositions. But after the piece went viral, the internet blew up in my face. Throughout my essay, I'd used the word "stalking"—as in "internet stalking"—something I considered a colloquial term at the time, but one that, given my car rental, people took quite seriously. So I was called a stalker, in the legal sense, and people wanted me to pay for it. Every five minutes, for more than two months, my phone buzzed with Twitter notifications and email alerts and actual phone calls and text messages from people who'd somehow tracked down my number.

The media team at HarperCollins initially wrote me fan mail about the piece, but when the tide turned against it on social media, they wrote me follow-up hatemail. My book editors said they'd talk to the media gals for me, but that my next book, a sequel that had been purchased as a package deal with the first, would not be promoted at all; they simply weren't sure how to market a young adult novel, they explained, without bloggers. They told me to "go for a walk," to "leave my computer at home" and "get some work done," not realizing that with their encouragement—in fact, because of what had felt like an ultimatum from them—the internet had become my work, and my home.

If someone sets your neighbor's lawn on fire, you might think of moving house or at least setting up some security precautions. I blocked people who wouldn't stop tweeting at me. I moved threatening emails, some of which told me to kill myself or contained Google Maps photos of my mother's house, to my spam folder. But my phone kept buzzing, and even when it didn't buzz, I unlocked it to see what people were saying about me. I'd begun to hate myself. I didn't know why—but I thought the internet could teach me.

Having never lost my mind before, I felt surprised by how persuasive madness was. Sites like Gawker, Jezebel, and the *Los*

Angeles Times ran articles about me that featured photos from my Instagram account—selfies that I'd taken with strangers' dogs, only they cropped the dogs out, so that it was just me, smiling like an overjoyed maniac. People I'd cooked dinner for in my home wrote posts on their blogs, analyzing the various microaggressions contained in my piece. I drank Grüner Velt-liner by the bottle, and swallowed Klonopin, and read everything bad that everyone said about me. Online, people's hatred made me sweat. IRL, people's love made me feel like a burden. I started to think it might be nice to die. Just for a little while. I would die, I decided, and then in the spring I'd get married to my fiancé, whom I loved. My mind wasn't working anymore.

One night I changed the passwords on all my various devices and started sawing at my wrist with a serrated knife. When I seemed to run out of space on one wrist, I switched to the other. But then the bloody crosshatching didn't match. The two wrists seemed uneven. So I tried to even them out.

At the psychiatric hospital, they took away my shoelaces and spiral notebooks. I met a woman named Marva who told me she was from outer space, but used to be a poet. The nurses forbade us to touch. But I would learn that patients found ways to comfort each other.

Marva barely spoke except to yell at us. But one day in group, she placed her forehead on the table and wept. All she wanted was a hug, she said. Holidays were approaching, and as part of our therapy that morning we were making paper snowflakes for the fake Christmas tree, which the nurses had erected in the day room. While the burly group therapist asked Marva if she needed a nurse, the other patients put down their safety scissors and stretched their hands toward her across the table, hissing Marva's name, until finally she looked up and wiped her eyes.

Marva. Marva! Pretend we're holding your hands right now—from Earth.

Unlike me, these women had real problems. Every day I listened, humiliated, as they recounted addictions to bath salts, or losing their teeth to domestic violence, or hearing Satan scream at them all day and generally being host to a brain that always felt on fire, and when the therapist finally called on me to share, I whispered what had brought me there, because I felt so chastened by the relative lushness of my life. I talked about finally becoming a young adult author, like I'd always wanted, and losing my precious career because of all these tweets, and how the mortification of it all had made my brain turn off.

Everyone else got to remain anonymous, I complained. But I had to exist, under my real name, my real face.

When I finally looked up, tears were rolling down my cheeks. But the other women were giggling.

"What?" I said.

The woman without teeth smiled.

"Marva thinks she's an alien," she said, "and you think you're a writer."

"But I am," I insisted. "I am, though."

"I am," Marva echoed.

Just then someone emitted a wild shriek, which sent everyone into fits—and at first I didn't recognize the sound of my own pealing laughter in the mix. It had been so long since I'd heard the noise. The therapist urged us to stop. "What's so funny?" she kept asking, and maybe we could have tried to explain it to her—the arrogance and self-delusion I'd just articulated—but instead we kept on laughing.

"And *I'm* famous!" the toothless woman shouted, and the rest of us howled until our teeth clacked and our eyes brimmed with water, and although I couldn't see them, I thought I heard them reaching for me, their fingers squeaking across the laminate tabletop—*Pretend we're holding your hands, from Earth*—and at least for that one moment, it felt like we were in on the same joke.

Prey

My obsession with animals preexisted any trauma in my life. As a five-year-old I wrote a fully illustrated book titled "Tigger Maskkir" (translation: "Tiger Massacre") about circus animals who revolt and eat the clowns. My teachers thought I was becoming deranged, due to a fracturing home life, but my mom explained that it had been going on since before the divorce. I interviewed neighbors about their dogs. I put my teddy bears and stuffed lions to bed every night under blankets of washcloths—I couldn't fall asleep until they were safely nestled together like Tetris pieces on the floor, covering every inch of carpet. I once stood for an hour with my face against the glass at Sea World, trying to make meaningful eye contact with a manatee. It never occurred to me that I was looking at a wild animal—my own reflection in the glass.

* * *

The opossum will play dead anywhere from a few minutes to several hours. At this time it cannot be provoked into moving. It can be kicked, poked and prodded, pinched or bitten without giving any signs of suffering. When the danger has passed, the opossum toddles away as if nothing ever happened.

—Ann Bailey Dunn, "Playing Possum,"
Wonderful West Virginia, July 2000

* * *

It was my first day of college. After unpacking, my mother and I went to the Habitat for Humanity sale and bought a broken futon for $20. We carried it back across the quad, up a few flights of stairs, and into my new common room. And then my back started hurting.

Flustered by our impending separation, my equally obsessive mother became fixated on the idea of getting me a massage. A fan of free massages, I traipsed alongside her through Harvard Square, scouting options.

Every place was booked except for a place called About Hair, which offered haircuts and massages in addition to selling antiques. The store was so stuffed with secondhand items that some had been arranged outside on the sidewalk. A dark-haired, sullen-looking girl around my age was keeping an eye on them.

"The masseuse isn't here today," she told me in a thick accent that sounded Russian. But what did I know? I'd come from the suburbs of Milwaukee, a place so uncosmopolitan that my supermarket had an aisle labeled "Ethnic" that consisted entirely of pasta.

Standing there on the historic cobblestones outside About Hair, across from the gorgeous campus onto which I'd labored so hard to trespass, I could not deny that I had made it far out of Wisconsin, but I felt like an imposter. Massachusetts was the epicenter of sophistication, in my mind. I wanted to be worldly, open-minded, unruffled by difference. So I told myself the garbage for sale at my feet was art, that whoever owned the store must be very interesting—and when a nauseatingly pale and bald and shockingly muscular man, around fifty or sixty years old, stepped out from behind the maybe-Russian girl and introduced himself as the owner, I told myself he was an artist. Blue veins pulsed across his scalp. He looked like an albino snake. But I dismissed the reptilian hissing in my mind as midwestern narrow-mindedness. When Duncan Purdy smiled at me, I smiled back.

"I told her the masseuse is busy today," the young woman mumbled, looking up at him with what appeared to be a mix of annoyance and fear.

He shook his head, smiling. "I can definitely fit her in."

"Was that place creepy or artistic?" I asked my mother as we walked away. My appointment was not for a few hours. There was still time to cancel.

"Cambridge is very artsy," she said, sounding distracted. Travel makes her nervous.

I nodded.

As I would later explain in my cross-examination, "I was trying very hard to be open-minded and not be sort of like a country girl, like a country bumpkin who didn't understand the big city."

* * *

Darwin's encyclopedic investigation of domesticated species revealed an intriguing phenomenon. From his survey of the animal breeding work, he found that domesticated mammals in general exhibit a suite of behavioral, physiological, and morphological traits not observed in their wild forebears. Today, the full set of these characteristics is known to include: increased docility and tameness, coat color changes, reductions in tooth size . . . [and] prolongations in juvenile behavior.

—Adam S. Wilkins, Richard W. Wrangham,
and W. Tecumseh Fitch, *Genetics*,
vol. 197, no. 3 (2014)

* * *

After putting my mom in a cab to the airport, I returned to About Hair, which was now completely empty except for Duncan Purdy, who led me down a short flight of stairs, past mountains of antiques, to a dark, windowless room. A stool stood next to the massage bed. There was an industrial canister of massage oil on top of it. The cap was off. "I'll give you a second to undress," he said, giving me a towel.

"What's this?" I asked.

"To cover yourself."

It was a bath towel. When hung vertically it fell from my clavicle to my upper thighs. At home, a family friend had often given me back rubs on a portable massage bed that she kept in her car. I had scar tissue in my shoulder from an injury sustained in middle school, while snowboarding for the first time in Michigan's Upper Peninsula. Befuddled by the injury, emergency room doctors in that small town had strapped my hand to my chest with an Ace bandage and discharged me for the six-hour car ride home. They thought it was dislocated. But over the next few days, the injury caved in and turned black. Milwaukee doctors performed surgery, put in pins, took them out, set me free. It still bothered me. The socket would not rotate and I had trouble lifting my hand above my head to blow-dry my hair. The family friend and I knew each other well, and even she covered me with a large bedsheet during massages.

But as I told myself, things were different on the East Coast.

*   *   *

Hognose snakes will often roll onto their back and play dead, going so far as to emit a foul musk and fecal matter from their cloaca and let their tongue hang out of their mouth, sometimes accompanied by small droplets of blood. If they are rolled upright while in this state, they will often roll back as if insisting they really are dead. It has been observed that the snake, while appearing to be dead, will still watch the threat that caused the death pose. The snake will "resurrect" sooner if the threat is looking away from it than if the threat is looking at the snake.

—Wikpedia (Original reference: G. M. Burghardt and H. W. Greene, "Predator Simulation and Duration of Death Feigning in Neonate Hognose Snakes," *Animal Behaviour*, vol. 36, no. 6 [1988])

* * *

I gave the account of what happened next so many times in preparation for what would become my sworn testimony that during the actual trial I could tell the story with no emotion whatsoever. I once admitted to the district attorney that while I never actually questioned my version of events, I'd relayed them so repeatedly that on good days the incident felt more like something memorized than a genuine memory.

"That's the point of testimony," she said gently.

I grew up with a narrow understanding of sexual assault: if it didn't include vaginal penetration (with knives on hand), it didn't count as rape. Until I found out what mattered legally, I didn't know how to categorize what had happened to me. I thought of it only in terms of his name: Duncan Purdy. In my gut it registered as a gross, sweaty thing that just lay there, coiled inside of me.

So here's how it went:

I lay facedown on the table underneath the bath towel. Duncan Purdy came in fully clothed and yanked my arms behind my back until the scar tissue in my bad arm crunched and I thought my shoulders would dislocate. He tugged the towel off, flipped me onto my back, and leaned over me in a 69 position so that his crotch was in my face and his face was in my stomach. I could hardly breathe. He was tugging at my tits and working his way down to my thighs.

Unlike the hognose snake (*Heterodon platirhinos*), I didn't shit myself or spit blood to make my lifelessness appear more real, but I did lie there frozen, with a detached sense of shock at my own paralyzed reaction, hating myself for being so stupid. *I followed him here.* I felt his nonerect penis through his pants at one point—a fact that stuck in my craw for a while afterward as one of the grossest parts—but I never saw it. And as the defense attorney said on the very last day of the trial, "It's not quite the same as the worst of the rapes that one can envision . . . for instance, if he had actually, you know, thrown somebody on the ground and raped them with his penis."

The details of which body parts he touched and in what order seem mundane and boring to me now—irrelevant except on the witness stand—though I still remember the overwhelming need to tell myself, over and over, that it wasn't bad so long as he wasn't looking at me—and he wasn't; he was staring at the ceiling the whole time. As he raked his rough fingers over my skin, slathering me in waxy-smelling oil, I clung to the notion that his contemplating something other than my body was polite and professional. Maybe I had been right to argue with my abhorrence and schedule the appointment.

Clearly he was not a masseuse because nothing he did felt good. But that didn't necessarily make him a pervert. After all, he wasn't looking at my body, which was exposed now on the table. He couldn't see where he was putting his hands, I reasoned. So he didn't meant to put them in my armpits, or in between my thighs. I was overreacting. It wasn't happening. He didn't mean to.

I had made an appointment for thirty minutes but the whole thing lasted forty-five. When it was over he left the room and I wrapped my arms around my legs to cover my nakedness. Then I looked up and saw a mirror, hung above me in such a way that if someone were lying naked on her back underneath it, you would be able to see clearly between her legs by looking at the ceiling. The room was dark and I hadn't noticed it before. But now my eyes had adjusted and I knew all my self-reassurances were bullshit. He hadn't been averting his eyes; he had been calculatedly watching from a strange remove.

I looked around the room, which upon further scrutiny resembled a wood workshop. There were no windows. The only light trickled in from upstairs through the slats on the door. It started to sink in that I was in danger. Nobody knew where I was except for my mother, who was on a plane. I looked up and there was Duncan Purdy with an industrial bucket and a sponge, blocking the doorway. I let him wash me. He cupped the sponge in his hand and shoved it inside of me multiple times. He fisted me basically, with a sponge in his hand, and I didn't make a sound.

"Go ahead and get dressed, I'll be upstairs," he said finally. "I'll be upstairs."

I wasn't sure if he'd actually repeated himself or if my head was creating an echo.

So I did, I put on my skirt and tank top—an outfit I remember only because Duncan Purdy's attorney would later ask me multiple times what I had been wearing that day, as if that had something to do with it—and met him by the cash register. In my mind, and in that moment, handing over the $48 my mother had given me was the last step to safety, the endpiece on a very close call. I hadn't yet wrapped my mind around the fact that getting out alive might not be the only issue, or that paying would hurt my chances of being taken seriously in a courtroom. At that moment, my instinct was to quietly survive.

"You have a very athletic body," he said, ringing me up. "Here's my card. If you come back, I'll give you a discount."

"Thank you," I said, feeling dazed as I slid his business card back across the counter. It was my only act of defiance that day. "Thank you so much."

As soon as the sun hit my face, I laughed. My knees were shaking and oil was dripping off the tips of my hair. I called my ex-boyfriend, who said, "Why in God's name didn't you leave?" Fifteen minutes later, I collapsed on the broken futon in my common room and gave one of my roommates the abbreviated version. "When I was ten, a man pulled down his bathing suit and masturbated at me," she responded. "In my opinion, it's best to forget about it."

The last person I told that day was my freshman proctor, a thirty-three-year-old man with braces who lived in the suite below ours. I pulled him aside at our dorm's ice-cream meet-and-greet and said, "I think I was molested." I wasn't sure what to call it.

"Were your breasts touched?" he asked sternly. I blinked at him, not knowing where to start. I wandered away and found myself in the sleep aid aisle at CVS. It was light out but I wanted to be dreaming. Fifteen minutes later, I was back in my dorm room, my eyes droopy from NyQuil, spending what would be the first of countless hours googling animal facts. "I need to erase it somehow," I wrote in my diary. So I started listing new things to be afraid of. An anaconda's prey ostensibly remains alive up until the digestion process. Moose are double-jointed and can kick in all directions while running up to thirty-five miles per hour. The cassowary, a shy bird that looks like a cross between a turkey and a velociraptor, and has sharp claws and a blue neck, and prowls Australian highways, and looms up to six and a half feet tall, not only exists, but can disembowel you with one sharp stroke. There were worse things out there than Duncan Purdy.

*   *   *

Tests of animal bones [at Chernobyl], where radioactivity gathers, reveal levels so high that the carcasses shouldn't be touched with bare hands.

—Mike Hale, "In Dead Zone of Chernobyl,
Animal Kingdom Thrives," *New York Times,*
October 18, 2011

*   *   *

I'd always been a social creature. But during those first two months of college, it became difficult for me to talk to other humans about anything except animals. As midterms rolled around, instead of studying I found myself in the bowels of the library researching wild beasts. Most afternoons, when I should have been talking to professors about stuff I failed to understand in class because I wasn't listening, I would aimlessly prowl the halls of the Natural History Museum, where I would read every single plaque five times, sometimes circling the space for hours before standing dazed under the whale skeleton—its baleen still intact and sprouting from its skull like a mustache. I preferred the clammy frenzy of my pointless research to class. Bettering myself, becoming credentialed, no longer obsessed me. In lecture, each professor's sonorous voice triggered a feeling of claustrophobia. But as I fantasized about life-and-death scenarios with various nonhuman species, his head became an unthreatening speck across the room, his voice a harmless, fanlike drone.

Over the next few weeks, I refocused my attention from the deadly beasts themselves to surviving hypothetical encounters with them. My know-how was gleaned from a combination of National Geographic videos, library books, and natural instinct. I even invented a game to distract and entertain myself during lectures: I'd flip to a fresh page, make it look like I was excitedly taking notes, and instead list as many scary creatures as I could, quizzing myself on the respective survival techniques. Then I'd check my answers against the answers in my diary, correcting myself in purple or blue pen—and occasionally chiming in on class discussion with evasive gobbledygook such as, "I totally agree with Bethany," or "Well, if you consider the text through a Foucauldian lens, the characters are actually emphasizing what they don't discuss. So what I'm interested in is the negative space in this book—what things have you guys noticed aren't happening?" And then they'd talk about that for a while.

Feral Hog: climb a tree √

Bear: play dead √

Great White Sharks: dig your thumbs into their eyeballs √

Crocodiles: run. | NO—*there's a flap in their gullet that seals to keep water out of their throat during the death spin, so you should kick down its throat and choke it with water before it drowns you.*

Coyote: kick its head √

Hyena: they hunt in packs so probably you will die. | *Correct, but you could wrestle.*

Lions: talk in a calm voice to it and try to appear large √

Rattlesnake: call 911 √

Boa Constrictor (or Anaconda): don't breathe. | *Well, yes, but also don't get caught in the first place. Also bite the tip of its tail as hard as you can.*

Moose: stay away! They're dumb and stompy. Protect head √

Tiger: I forget. | *Be quiet, hide, and if it pounces, run to where it won't land. Also FIGHT BACK.*

Piranha: don't bleed √

Mean Dog: kick it in the head √

Fox: kick it in the head √

Wolf: ? | *Need more books.*

Unbeknownst to me, I wasn't preparing to survive another attack, but rather to execute a counterattack of my own.

*　*　*

Feralization is the domestication process in reverse.

—Edward O. Price, "Behavioral Aspects of Animal Domestication,"
Quarterly Review of Biology, vol. 59, no. 1 (1984)

*　*　*

I finally told my mom what had happened after the school newspaper published an article announcing that local business owner Duncan Purdy had been accused of running a house of prostitution. It was Thanksgiving break and I was home for the long weekend.

Based on what was said in the article, undercover police officers had been staking out the joint for months. I imagined them watching through binoculars when I made my appointment. The sullen-looking maybe-Russian shopgirl on the sidewalk and others like her had been the masseuses, not him—and ostensibly she had turned me away because I did not physically qualify for the services she was there to perform. Or maybe she was trying to intervene—to save me from the man inside. Perhaps she knew what he was capable of. The idea that he might have done to others what he had done to me, combined with the fact that he was potentially a career criminal, somehow made my experience more real to me, and more categorically wrong.

"This is all my fault," Mom said, looking crumpled in the front seat. We were idling in the parking lot outside the mall. I kicked myself for not waiting to tell her until after we'd gone shopping; she hated the local shoe store even at the best of times. Now she was so upset we might not even end up going inside. "I set up the appointment. I should have known better."

"Can we please buy shoes?" I mumbled numbly. "Everyone at school is wearing those designer furry boots." I had called ahead to make sure the store had the fake version.

"Can I tell Daddy?"

I shrugged. Just imagining the conversation made my face burn.

She nodded, looking grave. "Your uncle knows people who could kill him. I think it's the Irish Mafia." She wasn't joking. Apparently we had connections.

"Mom. Come on."

I could feel her staring at me and wished there were something I could say to make her feel better that didn't involve us talking about it anymore. I was struggling with conflicting mind-sets: there was the need to be believed and heard, and simultaneously the need to acknowledge that my experience paled in comparison to some.

"Have you ever heard of the goliath tigerfish?" I tilted my head back, trying to keep the tears in with gravity. "They're humongous and have these awful, daggerlike buckteeth.

51

They're the only fish that don't fear crocodiles. They eat crocodiles, actually. Well, smaller ones, technically, but still."

"Can I hug you?" she asked.

I let her.

* * *

*Individual organisms in a community interact in many different
ways. An interaction may benefit both individuals, or the
interaction may benefit one organism to the detriment of the
other. An interaction between two organisms that benefits one
to the detriment of the other is an antagonistic interaction.*

—Allison N. P. Stevens, "Predation, Herbivory, and Parasitism,"
Nature Education (2010)

* * *

The victims' room at the district attorney's office is decorated
for the worst-case scenario. That is to say, it's decorated for children. The first time I told my story in its entirety, I was sitting
at the wrong end of a two-way mirror, in front of a Fisher-Price
table strewn with toys. Plastic farm animals and dump trucks.

They told me I was not the only girl. In addition to
prosecuting Duncan Purdy on charges of running a house
of prostitution, Assistant DA Melinda Thompson was also
building a separate rape case against him. Melinda explained
to me that although rape is often culturally defined by the
number of injuries a victim sustains while fighting off a dick,

Massachusetts's legal definition of rape is defined by three elements: "penetration of any orifice by any object; force or threat of force; against the will of the victim." I finally had a word to describe what had happened—"rape"—and as Mary Gaitskill described in her 1994 *Harper's* essay on "acquaintance rape": "the pumped-up version was more congruent with my feelings of violation than the confusing facts."

Jillian Gagnon looked like she could be my sister and had suffered a massage virtually identical to mine. (There were suspicions that Duncan Purdy had also hurt some of his sex workers, but none of them would, or really could, come forward due to fear of being deported.) Melinda explained that if I built my own case against Duncan, the judge and jury at Jillian's trial would not know about me, and the judge and jury at my trial would not know about Jillian. However, if I served as a "prior bad acts" witness at Jillian's upcoming trial, one jury would get to hear both stories.

I had never filed a police report. There was zero physical evidence. It had been months for me and years for Jillian since our respective massages. Any verdict would hinge almost entirely on accuser testimony. At the time, I never considered the possibility that a jury would not believe me.

As Melinda explained to me how the rules of evidence allow a jury considering a person's guilt in one crime to hear facts about a different crime that is similar to the charged crime as proof of the person's intent, system, or plan on the day he committed the charged crime—and how the jurors, in that scenario, aren't considering whether or not the accused is guilty of the "prior bad acts" crime, but instead hear about that crime as supporting evidence of his guilt in the charged crime—my head spun. By then my attention span had waned to the point that doctors at campus health services were recommending amphetamine salts.

But I'd watched enough National Geographic specials on group predation to know that deadly animals often hunt in packs. A few days later, I gave Melinda my answer. "Hyenas, wild dogs, lions—they're all social carnivores," I told her. "Even leopards—I mean, they're incredibly fast, but they rely on teamwork to survive."

If my drivel made her question having invited me to be a witness, Melinda didn't show it. Instead she listened attentively, arms crossed, nodding without any judgment—as if digressions about hyenas were common in the toy-littered victims' room. Then she shook my hand.

"Welcome to the pack," she said.

* * *

Prior to Jillian's trial, Melinda suggested it might be helpful to watch Duncan Purdy's prostitution sentencing. "Closure and stuff," she said. "No pressure."

She warned me the judge was "left-leaning," but I thought that was a good thing. Leftist intellectual principles had allowed me to feel so superior to my midwestern cohort. I didn't yet understand that in a country where the imprisoned population is predominantly made up of poor people, black people, and the mentally ill, criminals can also be victims. Hence, liberalism in the courtroom hinges first and foremost on second chances for the guilty—which makes sense, when you consider the constitutional principle behind American incarceration (rehabilitation), but not when you consider a victim's desire for revenge.

The man who got sentenced immediately prior to Duncan Purdy had been found guilty of hunting trick-or-treaters with a BB gun. I snatched a pen and notebook from my backpack and added "poachers" to my growing list of dangerous animals.

As I reviewed my notes on venomous snakes, one of the BB gun victims' parents stood up and read a victim's impact statement for the judge about how their eight-year-old had a BB pellet lodged near his heart that couldn't be removed or he would die.

"There's a chance it will slowly travel through his body and kill him anyway," the father said, clasping his wife's fingers, the printed statement shaking in his other hand.

But the judge wasn't paying attention. She gave the guilty man probation so quickly it was clear she'd made her decision even before putting on her robe. She explained that he'd had no priors, as if the BB thing had been a fluke.

Duncan stepped up.

In that moment, watching him stand before a lenient judge, I had the realization that humans are the most dangerous creatures. Of all the animals I'd studied, Duncan Purdy was the only one who'd actually hurt me. I watched his bald head shine greasily under the fluorescent lights and briefly regretted turning down my mother's offer of a hit man. I knew what happened to sex offenders in prison. And I wanted that for him.

The judge pushed a lock of hair behind her ear. She explained to the courtroom that, because of Purdy's previous crimes—which I learned ranged from drug possession to armed robbery—she planned to be slightly tougher on him than she had been on the poacher.

For the prostitution charges, she sentenced him to two years and one day.

Having covered criminal cases since then, I'm not surprised by her sentence. If anything, in retrospect, it seems pretty harsh. But at the time I felt shocked to learn that a man who'd wrestled immigrants into being his prostitutes would not be executed.

Still, I believed in the justice system. I trusted a jury to decide whether what had happened to me was wrong—I

wanted them to tell me what had happened, period. I thought
the circus ahead would at least bring closure, and stuff. I
thought I had noble intentions.

I was wrong about a lot of things.

*   *   *

Animals are ostracized by their pack for being mentally or
physically incapacitated, or for any other behavioral displays
that might threaten the survival of the group.

—Margaret Gruter and Roger D. Masters,
"Ostracism as a Social and Biological Phenomenon,"
Ethology and Sociobiology, vol. 7 (1986)

*   *   *

Girls, aside from those who became my closest friends, tried
to give me hugs and then disappeared forever, or judged from
afar. (While visiting me at college, my best friend from high
school took one look at the For Sale sign outside Duncan
Purdy's forlorn, now empty store and said, "God, I would have
left right away. What is *wrong* with you?") I was a teenager and
they were teenagers.

I lost a lot of friends that year, in part because I wanted
to tell everyone about the trial. Boys fetishized me, thinking
they could reintroduce me to sex, which I had never learned
to hate, or else they pulled my head to their chests, kissing my
hair, as if we were in a movie. Everyone tried their best to be

understanding, but the parts of our brain that develop empathy weren't all there yet, and even for the most adult person in the world, my problems and I were a burden. "You're too much," they said. And they were right; I was impossible.

But it wasn't just about Duncan Purdy. I was young and passionate and annoying and promiscuous. I ate nothing all day and made up for it at night. I smoked too much weed, slept with my friends and their friends, inspiring a lot of controversy everywhere I went. I was intolerable. I was exciting. People fell in love with my impetuosity but grew sick of my predictable selfishness. Then I fell in love with their unavailability, and we broke each other's hearts. As much as I wanted to break the mold of victimhood, my age and experience defined me.

Eventually, I whittled down my friend group to a combination of patient empaths, mentally ill people, basic masochists, and those who would, for whatever reason, listen to me digress at length about radioactive wolf bones. The story often burbled to the surface during inappropriate times: over lunch with new acquaintances, during a fight with a friend about something weird that I had done, or when a paper was due. In retrospect, these were potentially stressful moments, so it makes sense that they might have conjured stressful memories. But at the time, peers saw my decision to spill the beans over cafeteria brunch as manipulative and possibly unhinged, and they weren't wrong. Teaching assistants hinted that such confessions, when made while asking for an extension, seemed a little calculated.

"I couldn't tell if you were a bad person or the best person," a boyfriend from that period later confessed. "When you were talking about it, especially if we were fighting, it felt like the ultimate trump card."

In general, my audiences felt used by me, and as a storyteller I grew increasingly anxious about my power to unsettle. Writing this essay took its own toll; during early drafts I called an old friend and confidant to ask about the way I acted freshman year. He asked if this was an opportunity to air old grievances and I told him sure—I asked forgiveness, realizing only afterward that doing so was tantamount to apologizing for screaming after somebody had hit me.

Republishing it now is difficult, too. First I tried endlessly rewriting it before realizing I was stalling. The #MeToo movement was newly under way. But where I come from people remained skeptical. They worried that men are under fire. They talked about witch hunts and McCarthyism.

Literally days before I sent this version to my editor, a source for a different story I was writing would express incredulity and contempt for sexual abuse narratives in general. "Where were all these men when I was growing up?" she asked. "These girls are mad about something, but it isn't what they say."

Just because people on Twitter call you brave doesn't mean the world has changed.

* * *

When word got around the English department that I'd propositioned the boy who'd one day become my husband with a handwritten note in English 1A—"I am incredibly attracted to you," it said. "Want to have a 24 hour affair?"—one of the administrators called me into her office to ask if I had been sexually assaulted. The Duncan Purdy rape charges had been reported in the press, but as a victim, my name had been left out of it. She didn't know me and had drawn her conclusions solely from gossip about my sexual advances. Apparently in the wake of sexual trauma, many women seek to restore a sense of agency by becoming wanton. It makes them feel like they're controlling their bodies, even as it also opens them up to more abuse.

I didn't want to fit the stereotype. I told the rape expert to stop "slut-shaming" me.

"It's risk-taking behavior," she said.

"You're being sex-negative," I said. "I'm fine."

Then I walked to the library, where I used a stolen key to trespass onto the roof (something for which I could have been expelled) and smoked a joint (then very much illegal) and drank from a water bottle until the campus below swam from vodka and I nearly toppled off the edge to vomit on some trees. I called my mom, and when she asked, "What's wrong?" I told her I felt sad about the dodo bird, which became extinct because of its tameness, that friendly tendency to walk up to human strangers and expect the best.

* * *

I quickly developed such an incapacity for being alone, even while unconscious, that my roommates and male friends who had girlfriends would often wake to find me wrapped around them in their beds in the morning. They became justifiably angry, shaking me off and saying stuff about "boundaries," and I'd be like, "What are boundaries?" and then they would tell me to Wikipedia "boundaries." I wanted to tell everyone about the trial. I lured people in with my helplessness, exploited all their resources, slept with everyone I knew, and hurt people who trusted me. By graduation I would alienate almost everyone and burn out from self-sabotage.

On a visceral level, I also began to associate talking about what had happened with a certain degree of dissociation. The more I told the story, the more it was like I was talking about someone else. So was I still telling the truth of what had happened?

After Duncan Purdy was sentenced for prostitution, we had almost a year to build the rape trial against him. But instead of practicing my testimony in front of a mirror, as Melinda had instructed, or thinking about what I might wear on the stand to wordlessly convey my victimhood (I ended up impulsively ordering an ill-fitting beige polyester pantsuit from eBay and giving the matter no additional thought), I took out books from the library on fanged deep-sea creatures and memorized animal attack statistics (twenty-eight people in the United States died from dog bites in 2005).

When it came time to tell my story under oath, I put my hand on the Bible, spelled my full name for the court transcriber, and promptly panicked that the jurors in my peripheral vision would respond like my TAs when I referenced rape to get extensions and see my testimony as discomfiting and crafty. While the judge warned me to limit my remarks to "yes" or "no" when possible, I sweated copiously inside my little pantsuit, deliberating over how to make the jury believe me. As far as I could tell, most people's negative reactions to my confessional tendencies hinged on how uncomfortable I made them feel and to what extent they blamed me for that discomfort. So I steeled myself to give my responses frankly and without emoting, to be more convincing by appearing less invested. I didn't want to look like I was letting myself cry to sway them. I felt that any supposed performance on my part would be akin to lying under oath. So I answered the attorneys' questions casually, stony faced, and between each of my remarks I silently counted the number of constrictors I could remember offhand.

In other words, I did a horrible job.

Eleven out of twelve jurors believed Jillian and me, but one thought we were lying, which meant a hung jury, which meant a mistrial, which meant another whole trial, which could take one year or two, depending.

Boston was conservative enough that people yelled "faggot" and threw garbage at the movie screen when male actors hugged each other. I'd been stupid to operate under the assumption that by virtue of their East Coast residence, these strangers were somehow more sophisticated than my neighbors back home and knew better than I did. Invariably the next jury would have another unflappable skeptic—some guy who ostensibly harbored the same bigoted social defects of my high school's men's hockey team, a group of boys that had been known to categorize girls in terms of vaginal odor ("Was she fish or cheese?"). I knew how to talk to those people. I'd spent four years having sex with them.

The Massachusetts judge would be harder to control.

But I had a few ideas.

*   *   *

Domestic or "pet" pigs . . . will revert back to their wild state in a relatively short time. And that doesn't mean the next

*generation—the actual escapee will begin to grow hair and
tusks in the wild.*

—Eileen Stegemann, "Pigs Gone Wild: Feral Swine
Threaten New York State," *New York State
Conservationist*, October 2012

* * *

In preparation for the second trial, following some advice
from Melinda, I threw my Hillary Clinton–esque pantsuit in
the trash and riffled through my closet for something "sexy,"
settling on what I secretly referred to as my "party clothing":
a fitted white T-shirt and flared jeans that crept into my butt.
I knew I needed to wear something formfitting to the second trial to show how small I was—how easily overcome by
someone bigger and sicker. I also bought a headband to pull
my hair back, since I was planning to cry this time and figured
the jury sitting to my left should see my pretty face and bereft
expression.

I wore that outfit to the courthouse many times before
the trial actually began; the date kept getting pushed back
because Duncan Purdy kept getting sick or falling down on his
way to the courtroom. It was his legal right to ask for medical
attention.

Reading the transcripts now, it seems that Justice Diane
Kottmyer started to think that he was crying wolf, because
eventually she sent a patrol car to bring him in despite his

injuries. I remember he looked fine, albeit pale and veiny. I remember knowing he was a liar.

Here's what else I remember: camera phones were new then, and I took my first selfie in the hallway outside the courtroom to see what I looked like before going in. I remember, for the first time in ages, thinking I looked beautiful and knowing how dangerous that made me. I remember sitting on the witness stand and identifying Duncan Purdy with the blue-striped tie for the court as the man who'd done it, even though in my mind he was no longer anything more than a fleshless carcass—a sun-bleached rack of ribs eaten by vultures. I remember letting my hands shake on either side of the microphone so that the jury could see, so they would think that I was weak and fragile. I remember reshuffling the structure of my narrative without changing my story—this time, I approached the memory like I was writing it and, without changing the content, made cuts and structural changes for maximum impact. I started with the fact that he'd restrained my arms and that it had hurt.

Most of all, I remember being able to tell by Duncan Purdy's bored and blank expression that he didn't recognize me. (Melinda told me in the wings that although he pretended to know who I was, he kept confusing me with Jillian; she had the feeling that he'd done this sort of thing so many times he could not recall specific incidents.)

I'm trying hard to remember, because although I know I made myself cry and made the jury cry—and generally stirred the courtroom so that the defense attorney started his closing remarks by saying, "The first thing I want to talk to you about is Kathleen Hale's testimony, which just seemed very emotional, very heart-wrenching"—there is no record of what I actually said that day. The transcript ends just after my saying, "He gave me a towel." Comments thereafter read: "The audio abruptly stopped in the middle of direct testimony given by Ms. Kathleen Hale."

```
Q    Then what happened?
A    He gave me a towel --
     (End of audio - 3:26:50)
```

COMMENTS:
The information pages indicate that the case was heard in front of Justice Peter M. Lauriat. The judge was clearly a woman, whose name was not introduced. The cd did not come in JAVS formatting so there was no timestamping. Additionally, the audio abruptly stopped in the middle of direct testimony given by Ms. Kathleen Hale.

The transcript for that second trial cost me almost $400 (they charge per page) and I'm glad I bought it, even though my words aren't in it. From it, I learned that more than twenty individuals were disqualified from serving as jurors at my trial because they knew rapists or someone who'd been raped, or had been raped themselves, making the record of those proceedings a tender testament to the statistical likelihood of sexual assault.

One lady described how her young niece had been raped by a neighbor and then argued for her right to serve on the jury despite that, saying she was capable of objectivity despite what had happened to her loved one. Reading the transcript now, I have a feeling she was lying, but I thank her for it. Unbeknownst to me, a whole herd of people could identify with my experience and lost their voices as a result.

If anything, the absence of my testimony allows me to go on imagining that I contributed in large part to the actual jury's final verdict: they found Duncan Purdy guilty of rape.

*　　*　　*

The interesting thing about humans is that we're the only animals I can think of that collaborate not only for survival but for something we call justice.

—From my diary, Christmas 2007

*　　*　　*

At Duncan Purdy's rape sentencing, my roommates sat on either side of me and watched in horror as he flexed his butt muscles in front of us. He was handcuffed at that point and looked like a tied horse shivering its ass to shoo a fly. The aerobic display lasted so long that the three of us dissolved into snotty giggling messes and had to clutch one another, pretending to sob, so that we wouldn't look like psychopaths.

Judge Kottmyer glanced at us over her glasses, looked away politely, and asked if Duncan Purdy had anything to say for himself.

"Your Honor," Duncan said, still flexing his butt. "On behalf of myself and my family, I would just say that I regret the circumstances of this case and the burden that it's caused the Commonwealth and all the families concerned, myself and my family."

In the transcript, he then goes on to talk at length about how he can't go to prison because he needs to sell paintings.

Judge Kottmyer—whose disdain for Duncan Purdy had become increasingly evident throughout the trial—finally cut him off, responding, "What I see, Mr. Purdy, is that you don't comprehend and you're not remorseful—"

"I am," Duncan Purdy muttered, and dropped onto his seat like a petulant teenage boy.

"You don't comprehend that, in fact, what the evidence shows here, viewed against the backdrop of your entire record in terms of deriving support from prostitution, is that you—you have acted as a *predator*."

"I respect your opinion—"

"Stand up, sir," she boomed.

In Massachusetts at the time, the minimum sentence for rape was probation. But Judge Kottmyer sentenced Duncan Purdy to seven to ten years.

That night, my friends threw a party entitled, "Seven to Ten Years, Seven to Ten Beers." Everyone got raucously drunk and made sexual advances that somehow seemed within the bounds of friendship. To us, life was a series of soaring tragedies and once-in-a-lifetime bacchanalia, piggybacked on one another. College is the only human kingdom I can think of, other than prison, where drugs and violence and sex commingle on a single plot of land.

The next day, it was as if none of it had happened. My friends laughed and quoted popular television shows. I scanned their faces and realized with a lurch that it was over.

* * *

A few weeks before I first published this essay in 2014, a representative from the Commonwealth of Massachusetts called to remind me that Duncan would be up for parole. (The representative also encouraged me to update any restraining orders I might have, because Duncan Purdy had recently changed his name to Duke One Blood True Blood—"A.k.a. Mr. Blood," the guy said, sighing. "So at least anyone who meets him after his release will know he is a fucking lunatic.") Duke didn't get out, but years later, when I sat down to revise the piece, again, for this book, my dad dramatically arrived at my front door with "big news." Again, Duke was up for parole. Again, my parents promised me they'd fight it.

I learned they'd long ago changed the phone numbers on file with the Massachusetts Commonwealth so that I wouldn't have to talk to anyone or even think about it. I knew that their persistent involvement, their obvious preoccupation with Mr. Blood's life and punishment, stemmed from a place of love— but it also riled something in me. It revealed a picture of me in their minds as hysterical and helpless and too easily triggered to be tasked with adult matters. It reminded me that I had, in fact, acted that way for a long time.

So I told my dad to leave it, to open the barn doors, set free the animals, and let the tigers eat the clowns.

"That's quite a metaphor," he said.

But going forward he agreed to care as much or as little as I did about this thing, which, although persistent in my mind, felt small to me.

So I ignored the unknown callers with Boston area codes, presumably phoning with some update about Mr. Blood, because I didn't want to talk about it anymore. But I stopped fighting his release. As I write this, I actually don't know if he is free, or still behind bars. I don't check—not because I'm scared that he's out, but the opposite: I'm scared he's in. It's hard not to feel at least a little guilty for putting another human being in a cage.

That's probably not an attractive thing for a victim to say. But I've never been the perfect victim—the girl who starts off weak and becomes unwaveringly strong. I believe in Jillian Gagnon, and I am glad we teamed up to fight Mr. Blood, and I support the verdict she won for herself. But whatever part I played, I think I put Duncan Purdy in prison for reasons that had little to do with him, or what he'd done.

* * *

In elementary school, a young man, who'd later be arrested for raping and beating women in the neighborhood, crept into my backyard and beckoned to me with his penis. At nine, a teenaged cousin of mine, who turned out to assault members of my extended family, liked to initiate games with me in the back of his parents' minivan, where we'd place our fingers higher and higher on each other's thigh. When I was only twelve, I smiled at someone's dad at Blockbuster, and on his way out, he pressed himself against me, cupping my butt through my gym shorts. I was standing right next to my mother at the time but didn't say anything because I didn't want her to yell.

71

And those are just highlights. That's what happened before I went through puberty and turned into a blond babe in a push-up bra.

For centuries African villagers killed elephants for profit and endured grisly elephant attacks. They took tusks and woke at night to stampedes. Scientists used to think the elephants' bloodlust came from actual hunger—that human casualties were an unintentional effect of the animals' desperation to find food or water. But it turned out the elephants weren't starving. They had more than enough to eat and drink. Over time, humans uncovered the truth: the animals wanted revenge.

The humans who had murdered their mates and their children for ivory were etched into the elephants' memories, and under cover of darkness, they trampled anyone who looked like their attackers.

Perhaps if I'd not been sexualized so young, Duncan Purdy might not have fazed me. Maybe if I'd gone through life untampered with, I would have let this one slide. Instead a lifetime of gross and confusing experiences—all of which seemed wrong once the opportunity to react had passed— pressed against me like that man at Blockbuster.

Duncan Purdy wasn't the first man to sexually frighten me. But he became my first opportunity to do something about all of it.

It's impossible for anyone, I think, to seek revenge—to set out to change another person's life for good—without at least subconsciously drawing on her past frustrations and humiliations. In so many cases the person on trial becomes a proxy for everyone else who got away with it. I think that's what makes victims so mistrusted.

And so dangerous.

THE COURT: I have one more question, sir. Have you, or to your knowledge has any member of your family or close friend ever either been accused of or the victim of a sexual offense?

THE JUROR: Yes.

THE COURT: And why do you say yes?

The JUROR: My grandfather was accused.

THE COURT: I have another question,
sir. Have you, or to your knowledge has any
member of your family or close friend ever
either been accused of or the victim of a
sexual offense?

THE JUROR: My sister, but she never
went to anybody about it.

THE COURT: All right.

THE JUROR: That was told to me in --

THE COURT: I'm sorry?

THE JUROR: That was told to me in
private.

THE JUROR: My mother was raped twice.
I was a victim of a sexual assault in high
school.

THE COURT: All right.

THE JUROR: Can anyone say no to this?

I Hunted Feral Hogs as a Favor to the World

I first became obsessed with feral hogs during my short-lived tenure as an MFA student at Southern Illinois University in Carbondale, a place where more than a dozen people died each year from pit bull attacks, and brown recluse spiders slept inside people's shoes (their bites cause necrotic wounds that can take years to close)—and to top things off, every spring a pestilence known as ant season descended on the region. Come April, I found so many ants swarming inside my mailbox that it looked like the metal was breathing. In class, I'd be gesticulating to punctuate some pretentious literary observation and would suddenly notice ants crawling out from my shirtsleeves.

I tried traps, into which the trespassing ants marched single file while I laughed at them like a heartless overlord. But more armies arrived to break apart and hoist onto their backs the carcasses of flies I hadn't noticed while cleaning house. They seemed impossible to kill.

Then one night outside my window I heard the trash cans get knocked over—followed by an animal scream, which sounded so impossibly human that I dashed outside with a hammer thinking someone was being murdered, only to see the trees behind my house bend apart and snap back together, swallowing up whatever large and whining beast had eaten up my garbage. The next morning I found a giant pile of shit in the driveway, and when I sent a picture of it to a hunter I knew, he texted back, "Hogs."

By happenstance I'd recently watched a program on the Discovery Channel called "Hogs Gone Wild," a special on feral hogs, which I learned could grow up to eight feet long and four feet at the shoulder (google "Hogzilla" for a better sense of these nightmarish proportions). Between their hairy faces and beady eyes and long meaty bodies, they reminded me of the Rodents of Unusual Size from *The Princess Bride*. When I read about their tendency to mate and give birth in residential swimming pools, and to murder people's poor sweet little doggies, I felt alive for the first time in months.

Ever since my freshman year of college, I had daydreamed about defending myself against wild animal predators. Now I sat by the back door clutching my hammer, yelling at ants and waiting for hogs to come eat my body. It wasn't how I'd pictured my early twenties: hiding out the recession in my little MFA program, at the proverbial bottom of the food chain. Maybe if I could triumph over these disgusting pigs, the rest of my life would fall into place. So I devoted myself to the task of getting to know my enemy.

* * *

Historians think feral hogs were probably first introduced into the American wilderness during the 1600s and 1700s by European explorers and settlers. Some of the immigrant pigs had been born wild, brought over from their native home of England, where they prowled countrysides and were hunted by gentlemen. Others arrived as domesticated pigs, and had immigrated to America to become pork, but were either set free or escaped, and began breeding like crazy.

Back in 2005, the *New Yorker* described the wild hog as an "infestation machine" ("Suddenly, feral swine are everywhere"). Female wild hogs go through puberty as young as three or four months old and give birth frequently, with a gestational cycle of only sixteen or seventeen weeks. Twice annually they can produce large litters of up to 14 piglets—which means that the oldest documented female feral hog, who survived to the age of fourteen years old, may have produced up to 392 offspring over the course of her lifetime. Those offspring, in turn, were biologically capable of generating as many as 153,664 piglets. That's more than one tenth of a million pigs in just one feral family.

By 2012, when I was in grad school, they had become such a destructive invasive species that municipal governments in places like Arkansas had set up "pork chopper" laws, allowing hunters to shoot down feral hogs from helicopters. In Texas, the *Guardian* reported a full-blown "aporkalpyse," in which residents massacred the animals with machine guns and night-vision goggles. In 2013 alone, Texans managed to kill as many as 750,000 pigs. But even that wasn't enough to keep up with the birth rate, and hunters left behind an estimated 1.8 to 3.4 million feral hogs.

I should have been writing my novel, or whatever it was I thought I was working on, but I couldn't stop thinking about hogs, so I spent ant season writing, maybe, eleven stories—but basically the same one over and over. My MFA cohort responded with characteristic vitriol, scrawling three-page-long single-spaced critiques that ended with sound conclusions like, "There's not even a story in this story, just facts about pigs," and "Kathleen, I feel like your writing is consistently preoccupied with hog sex and hog violence," and "Kathleen, maybe you should see a therapist"—scathing truths that exposed my fiction for what it was: a symptom of my hog madness.

Finally, after months spent fielding criticism and shaking spiders from my sneakers and fearing pigs I'd never actually seen, I dropped out of my MFA program. I'd failed at graduate school and at being a writer, and had given up on all of my life's dreams. But there was still one concrete and good thing that I could contribute to the world. And that was murdering a feral hog.

* * *

I flew into West Palm Beach airport in early June with my friend Sarah McKetta, whom I call McKetta, because otherwise, when I address her in public, every woman's head turns. McKetta is, incidentally, a vegan. But here we were, off to hunt for meat in Okeechobee, Florida.

Before we left for the hunt, I called up Stephen Dubinski, a seasoned feral hog hunter, to get a better understanding of America's hog problem. "The rate of reproduction is unbelievable," he explained. "More people are getting involved in harvesting them. But it just seems like a losing battle. It's just crazy and worrisome, especially when they're near little kids. It's dangerous. I don't have any idea of how to deal with it except more killing."

I asked him what feral hog overpopulation looks like up close.

"I haven't seen any type of wildlife explode the way these hogs have," he responded. "From one tree stand, one afternoon, I saw over seventy piglets, all sizes. All the ones I've shot over the years have been pregnant." He added, "We lay the fetuses on the grass. Other pigs will come and eat them. Nothing's there in the morning."

When I told him that I'd signed up for a guided hunt in Okeechobee and planned to kill a feral hog as a mitzvah to the world, Dubinski said he didn't know what a mitzvah was but that he hoped I'd get out unscathed.

"Aim for the shoulders," he told me. "Kill as many as possible."

*   *   *

The streets leading from West Palm Beach airport to Okeechobee are named after citrus fruits, brands of alcohol, dead presidents, and politically incorrect terms for Native Americans. Moss hangs from the trees and power lines alike. Roads are lined with huge, toothy plants that look like monsters. En route to our hotel we braked for a group of hunchbacked feral hogs, screaming as they scuttled like humongous rats across the highway's sweltering pavement. I waited for the pigs to disappear before driving over the speed bump of excrement they left behind.

After dropping off our bags we crossed the parking lot to eat at Applebee's.

"Is there anything fun to do around here?" I asked our waitress as she seated us.

"I've been here since 2003," she said pleasantly. "There's nothing."

"We're going hunting tomorrow," I said.

She nodded. "People around here are always hunting something."

On the ride over to the hunting grounds the next morning, we blasted the air-conditioning but couldn't stop sweating.

Entering the dirt road leading to the eight hundred acres surrounding Ron's Guide Service felt like entering Jurassic Park. There were multiple gates and warning signs with terrifying beasts on them. Dust blew in our eyes as we ducked out of the car. It was time.

"You my ten o'clock?" a man in jeans called to us. He was standing under a metal lean-to, surrounded by meat hooks, wiping off his hands. I wouldn't call him a handsome man. His skin looked like beef jerky, but he seemed healthy. I felt safe around him, like he would save me if a hog got its horns into my stomach, even though later he would have me sign a liability waiver that made it clear, in no uncertain terms, that I could die and that was my business.

"Is Big Mama here?" I asked.

I had spoken to Big Mama on the phone a few days prior about appropriate hunting gear. "Wear anything except booty shorts. It's Florida, so the bugs get in," she said. She kept calling me "honey child" and asking me to speak up because she was deaf from "all the crossbows." I didn't yet understand the crossbow reference. But I liked Big Mama.

"Big Mama's not here," the guy said, shaking his head. The look on his face suggested that Big Mama might be dead. "But I'm Joe."

Joe led us to a locker full of guns and asked which ones we wanted. McKetta explained that she wouldn't be hunting, just watching, because she was a vegan. "What's 'vegan'?" asked Joe. McKetta spent a while explaining the dietary restrictions she subscribed to, then told us that if we needed her she'd be taking pictures of the alligator heads scattered on the ground. Before she walked away, Joe had her sign another waiver. I was starting to feel nervous.

"How many waivers are there?"

"Enough so it's not my fault."

I stared at the guns.

"Joe, can I talk to you about some feelings I'm having?"

I proceeded to explain to a now very confused Joe that in addition to concerns for my own safety, hog-wise, I worried that if I took off into the Floridian jungle with a gun, I might accidentally shoot myself in the face or kill McKetta. I explained that I wasn't exactly what you might call "graceful," or "athletic," or "coordinated," and had fallen over just that morning while putting on my denim overalls—and that falling over while putting on pants was actually something I did pretty often.

Joe handed me a handgun, and I handed it back. So he suggested a crossbow, and I was like, "Are there any laws in Florida?" and Joe was like, "Not really, that's why pedophiles go to live in the panhandle after they're finished up with prison," and I was like, "Whoa."

Joe became exasperated. "Are you going to kill or not?"

I sighed. "I do want to kill, Joe, really I do."

"Well, then pick a weapon!"

I racked my brain for other armaments, ones that would not have a chance of fatal ballistic error, but could think only of cartoonish weaponry, like swords and war hammers.

"Would a knife be too crazy?" I whispered.

Stephen Dubinski had gotten weird on the phone when I asked him about knife slaughters. He told me that knife kills were too up close and personal, even for him—said by the man who killed pregnant animals and used their unborn babies to bait other animals he wanted to kill.

"It just feels slightly safer to me, in terms of collateral damage," I said to Joe. "Given that there's no trigger to accidentally pull."

Joe disappeared into the small bathroom/kitchen attached to the lean-to and returned with a rusty knife that still had mayonnaise on the blade. Then he yelled, "Vegan!" and McKetta returned, and Joe dragged two hunting dogs out of their kennels and put them in separate cages on the back of the truck we'd be driving. One of the dogs hooked its hind legs around the outside of the cage, not wanting to get stuffed inside.

"Can I pet them?" I asked.

"Pet Sadie," Joe said, indicating the dog who did not seem to have truck-related PTSD. "Spoon's demented."

I petted Sadie and then followed McKetta into the truck. "How long have you been doing this?" I yelled to Joe over the engine. There were no seat belts, and the terrain was so rocky that I had to squat a little over my chair and clutch the bottom of the seat with my nonstabbing hand so as not to get tossed overboard.

"My entire life," he said. "Twenty-five years."

"So that sign back at the meat-hook place," I said to Joe. "The one on the wall with various animals and amounts of money—?"

"The price list?"

"Yeah. What was the thing about 'Dogs: $2000'? Is that if people want to buy the dogs?"

Joe laughed.

"Wait," I said. "Can people pay to kill the dogs?"

"Why?" he asked, sounding interested. "Do you want to?"

I felt like passing out. It was hot, the truck was lurching over holes, and despite having deliberately chosen a weapon that would be safe, I was now worried about stabbing myself with the knife clutched in my free hand, soon to be my killing hand.

"There's one," Joe said. "Do you see?"

McKetta and I shook our heads.

He stopped the truck, climbed down, and unlatched Sadie's cage. She leaped out, bounding through the tall grass like a happy dog from a dog-food commercial—only skinnier and probably abused.

"Do humans get hurt on these trips a lot, or just dogs?" I asked Joe when he got back in the driver's seat. We began trailing Sadie in the truck.

"That's why we had you sign the waiver."

"But it's not bad or anything, right?"

"Sometimes it's real bad."

"You're going to shoot it before I stab it, right?"

"Nah, I'll just hold its legs."

"But what about its tusks?"

"You need to be careful. That's why you signed the waiver."

McKetta looked back and forth between us. "Why does he keep bringing up the waiver?" She turned to Joe. "What did I sign?"

"Simmer, Vegan," Joe said. "The guys who get hurt are the crazy ones. They jump off the truck onto the hog's back, then they get gored. Stomach outside the body."

"But they live?" I said.

I watched Sadie disappear into the trees, chasing something we couldn't see or hear.

"Yeah. But they're not the same." Joe shook his head. "War turns men into animals."

"What?" McKetta said.

Just then Sadie barked. She'd found something worth mentioning in the thick, dank foliage.

Joe slammed to a stop, and hustled out of the truck to unlatch Spoon, who burst from his cage, frothing at the mouth. I clutched my knife and followed, McKetta at my tail. Joe ran ahead and was immediately swallowed up by the jungle. We could hear him barking along with the dogs and screaming, "Cowabunga!"

We looked at each other before following in his footsteps. "Joe?" we called in unison. As we pushed through the tropical leaves, I spotted wiry hair dashing through the grass—and then something huge charged us.

"Hog!" I yelled, throwing an elbow over a low branch and swinging my leg up like a monkey, trying not to cut myself in the process. By the time McKetta looked up and saw the feral pig coming, and before Joe even yelled, "Watch out!" I was fully inside the tree. Mortal fear had briefly transformed me into a gymnast.

Below me, McKetta screamed and hurled herself into a ditch. The hog flew by, and I jumped down to chase it. Only in its wake did I realize it had no tusks. The hog was a sow. A procreation machine.

"Come on!" Joe shouted, so I followed his voice, pushing aside high brush. I found him gripping the huge and hairy pig by her hind legs. Spoon had her by the face. The hog was screaming—not the high-pitched squeal that I would have expected, but a desperate, drawn-out grunt. She must have weighed two hundred pounds.

"Do it!" Joe said.

I threw a leg over her and lined up the tip of my knife with her armpit. Spoon was struggling to keep her head still, and even though I could see the sow's fangs glistening in the melee, I could tell she was in pain. For a second I didn't think I could do it. None of my fiction writing had prepared me for this pivotal moment of reckoning (or for anything, really, but that's a different story). I considered that God had made this hog and me in His image and that she didn't deserve this unnatural death.

But then I stabbed the shit out of her.

I hit the heart on the third try. Then I stabbed her three more times. Later, when we took the heart out of her body, I saw that I had nailed it. Twice.

McKetta whooped, wiping sweat off her face. "That thing was a monster."

"I'm a monster," I said.

"Fuck off," Joe yelled. It took us a second to realize he wasn't talking to us but to Spoon, who wouldn't let go of the sow's face.

"Spoon, get!" Joe swatted at him with a stick, but Spoon, as promised, was demented and wouldn't let go.

"I said get!" Joe said, kicking Spoon in the head with his steel-toed boot. Spoon yelped, and McKetta and I held our breath as Joe kicked him again and again.

In retrospect, I think Joe hoped that I would buy the sow's head, have it stuffed and mounted and pay extra, or whatever. He needed Spoon to let go—to stop destroying what he could potentially sell.

Just when I thought Spoon might die, he growled and backed away from the corpse.

"You want the meat?" Joe asked me.

I shook my head. I told him I was sure she tasted great, but I didn't have room for a whole hog in my hotel mini fridge. So McKetta found a nearby church that took all sorts of animal meat donations—even raccoons and armadillos. "Hog wild," the person on the phone said, laughing. "Praise the Lord."

Back at the meat hooks, the next group of would-be hunters waited for their turn with Joe. They were from a nearby Baptist church. When they learned I'd stabbed the sow that Joe was gutting, they nearly lost it, hooting and hollering. "Let me take your picture," the preacher said. I realized that the only females in our vicinity were McKetta, me, the dead sow, and Sadie, who was now passed out from heat exhaustion in her cage.

"Is there anything here I can pet?" I asked. There was blood on my hands and I needed to hug something, like a therapy dog or potentially a life coach.

"Here's a puppy," the preacher said, handing me their hunting dog in training. She was small and soft and licked my face.

"You want the hog head?" Joe asked, hosing blood down a drain. "I got Spoon off it in time. There's hardly a nick on either ear. We can do it up for you nice."

"Let me get you the head as a present," McKetta offered. "I'm proud of you."

"Really?"

"Yeah, that was scary. I thought it would bother me but it didn't."

Joe grabbed another knife and skinned the sow so that her hide dangled inside out around her face. Then he snapped the skull from the spine and dropped the whole thing into a large brown paper bag. Blood seeped through.

"It's a head bag," Joe explained. "We'll write your name on it, and that way they'll know to call you."

"But when I get it in the mail, how will I know if it's the right head?"

"Who cares?" he said.

Joe was right. Feral hogs are a bunch of monsters. They're all the same, and they all deserve to die.

Cricket

Miss Georgia wept as if her entire family had died. She hugged her bouquet of thorny roses and was swallowed up in a group hug by her enemies. While they worked the crown into her slightly exhausted-looking curls, like some kind of crack sniper I focused my binoculars on the contestants who didn't even make it past the preliminaries. After a year spent preparing for the oldest beauty pageant in the nation, they had lost before the competition even began. They'd spent tonight sitting on the sidelines, smiling for hours just in case the cameras spotted them, wearing white gowns, looking like sacrificial lambs. Now they seemed euphoric, almost orgasmic, over Miss Georgia's win—but in a poised way. The woman sitting next to me shouted to her friend, "Miss Alaska is a dog!" I caught her eye but said nothing to defend my fellow woman.

I arrived at Miss America a very different person—a principled person, the sort who would have defended Miss Alaska, who was only nineteen. But watching women parade around a stage in their bathing suits, and toss batons, and clog, which I'd never heard of prior to this event, had changed me.

And now, here's what I thought: forty of the contestants were dogs, five were so-so, seven were hot, and I fell somewhere toward the bottom of the pack. When I came to Atlantic

City, I considered myself self-confident, pretty, and young. Now, I saw my body as an assemblage of component parts, a patchwork of wrinkling imperfections in need of ironing and toning and implants and paralytic injections—anything to freeze time. I'd become so detached from my own body—from bodies in general—that on my bus ride back to New York City after the pageant, I would look out my window to see firefighters spraying a charred minivan—their boots slipping on what at first appeared to be mushy bits of orange pumpkin meat, but turned out to be the flayed remains of human flesh—and feel, basically, nothing.

But for now, I turned my attention to the stage. Ombre purple and coral-pink panels dappled with digital stars. Curtains shimmering electric blue. A cartoon mermaid's natural environment. On stage left stood a gigantic golden statue, like the one at the Oscars. Only it looked like this one had breasts. I couldn't really tell. My seat was pretty bad. The ladies next to me kept going on about Miss Alaska and how "that yellow bikini she wore on night one made her look like an albino dog—haha!" On the big screen, I caught a glimpse of Miss Alaska, smiling brightly like she'd won and hugging all the other losers, their heads tipped back in jubilee, teeth bared.

Primates smile to submit; if a beta meets an alpha in the wild, he shows his teeth to indicate his inferior rank. It's called a fear grin. Sociologists say human women smile more than men because their lower social status motivates deference. They smile to indicate attentiveness to the needs, goals, and accomplishments of those who are more powerful.

If I'd learned anything in Atlantic City, it's that girls were expected to lose like winners and win like losers.

Miss Georgia fingered her crown, continuing to sob.

Like her, my dissolution into madness started with roses.

* * *

A week earlier, I'd taken the Academy Bus from Manhattan to the Trump Taj Mahal. The ride had cost $40, a full $15 more than the regular Greyhound. But I'd decided to "go fancy," in the hopes that eavesdropping on what's casually known as the "casino bus" would give me a sense of "the scene" in Atlantic City.

"The devil is in the details," I wrote to my editor, requesting the extra money. "And details pay dividends ☺."

Unfortunately, I had chosen to travel on Labor Day, so the bus was completely empty except for me and four other people, two of whom were speaking Yiddish, and two of whom were annoying mumblers. Over the course of the two-and-a-quarter-hour trip, all I could make out from the English speakers was "I think that girl is listening to us." I wrote it down.

As we pulled into the casino's unexceptional carport (white overhang, concrete pillars, a booth just inside the door that looked like the check-in desk at an airport), I was excited to learn from our driver that the pointlessly expensive bus tickets came with thirty credits' worth of Trump Dollars.

"Luck be a lady tonight!" I said.

When the bus driver didn't seem to "catch my drift," I hummed the first few bars of that big solo from *Guys and Dolls* and danced off to the beat of my own drum. I was a confident lady!

After that, I was on my own in Atlantic City.

To cash in my voucher, I first had to navigate a sea of blackjack tables, free drinks, and blinking slot machines. Dick Clark Productions, which puts on Miss America as well as the Academy of Country Music Awards and *So You Think You Can Dance*, had denied me a press pass. (An inside source said it was because the people in charge found my writing "inappropriate," which is totally fair.) But I was hoping to get the exclusive scoop from burned-out employees using my untested charm.

The lady behind the desk watched as I scanned her breasts for a name tag. In my mind, I was a sly, charismatic investigative reporter, off to prove that Miss America was what I had decided it was: an empowering feminist exploration of the beauty myth, in which contestants adjusted their appearances and personalities to game a sexist system.

"Hi . . . Chantelle," I crooned.

But she didn't like that. So I asked in a businesslike voice whether she'd been experiencing an influx of people for the Miss America pageant. Had it been overwhelming, I wondered, to deal with a larger-than-usual crowd?

When Chantelle didn't answer, I asked again, thinking maybe she hadn't heard me.

"I heard you," she said, handing me my official Trump Card. "No one cares about Miss America. There's no one here for that. They're here to gamble. Welcome to Atlantic City."

Undeterred, I carried my swipe card full of Trump Dollars past an old man crying alone at the craps table, and sat down at a slot machine called "Vibrant Rose" (or rather, "Vibrant 🌹"). I had gone to college and everything, but I couldn't figure out how any of this worked, so I asked the guy next to me for help, raising my voice a little to be heard over the dinging of slots. But he kept his eyes on his machine, gripping its handle as if clinging to life.

"Hello?" I shouted, poking helplessly at my console, until suddenly a woman reversed toward me in one of those wheelchairs with a bicycle basket and handlebars and offered to help.

"Thank you!" I said.

But then she stood up from her wheelchair, and I screamed, not knowing whether to fall on my knees in the face of what appeared to be a miracle (she can walk!) or shake myself awake. (The negative reaction to that 2000 Super Bowl commercial featuring an ambulatory Christopher Reeve is a testament to how shocking this can be.)

The woman looked confused, so I explained I had thought she was paralyzed, which is when I learned that her little vehicle was not a wheelchair at all but a "scooter."

"You rent them from any of the casinos for twenty-five dollars," she said. "It's easier than walking or standing."

Without taking a single step, she slid onto the chair next to mine and walked me through the embarrassingly easy process of cashing in my Trump Dollars. I noticed that her card was different from mine and attached to a lanyard on her belt. I couldn't tell whether the lanyard was an actual electrical cord, or a way to keep the card handy and avoid losing it, or simply a fashion statement, but regardless, it seemed to allow her to sit back and play without even having to press the green SPIN button on the machine.

Looking around, I saw that many of the gamblers wore such lanyards, connecting them to their slots as if by IV.

I pressed SPIN, and within seconds my balance had dwindled from $30 to $9. I struggled to mirror my neighbors' vacant calm.

But then, out of nowhere, Vibrant 🌹 started ringing and wouldn't stop.

"What's happening?" I screamed, shaking the scooter woman's shoulder. But part of me already knew: I was winning—I had won! I tried to get the scooter woman to dance with me, but she stormed away to her scooter and scooted off (jealousy tears women apart). Images of blue and red diamonds and gold coins exploded across my screen to the tune of our national anthem.

After cashing out the $220 in winnings, an insane thought entered my mind: "With this fortune, I will never have to work again."

I texted my husband, explaining how casinos are actually just like ATMs, except it's not your money. His response—something about "this is how it starts, I love you, don't give in to the allure of Lady Luck, blah blah blah"— did not sink in.

I proceeded to go full "money crazy." I purchased an enormous pretzel for $6. I bought a hat made out of balloons. I paid an elderly conductor to physically push me all the way to my hotel in a carriage, because you can do that in Atlantic City. While the old man panted and moaned, I counted my remaining cash, thinking, "No wonder people want to be Miss America!"

Whoever won the pageant would receive $50,000*— enough for 8,333 pretzels!

---

* In scholarships, but still.

If you had told me then what the rest of that week held in store—feral cats, possible tetanus, a dead body in a bathroom stall—I might have seen reason.

I might have taken my winnings and gone home.

* * *

The Claridge Hotel, known as, "Home of Miss America," had a fancy restaurant called the Twenties, which was in fact decorated in the style of the eighties, with brown geo-print carpeting and black chairs.

On the morning of the first round of preliminaries,* I sat there for hours, hoping to catch sight of one of the contestants. (I'd heard a rumor they all slept on the fourteenth floor.) Instead I saw lots and lots of "Teen Misses." One told me she had come to "get tips from watching" her idols.

Mostly, I talked to my waitress, Lee.

"To tell the truth, they're getting to be pretty freaky," she said of the actual Miss America contestants whom she'd waited on so far. "I'm like, you're Miss America, you're supposed to be nice. But they don't even leave tips. And they smile, smile,

---

* The weeklong competition began with three nights of preliminaries, allowing attendees who showed up in person to watch every one of the fifty-two talented young women (one for each state in the union, plus Washington, D.C., and Puerto Rico) perform in bikinis and evening gowns before the group was narrowed down to fifteen for the official TV broadcast.

smile, and, yeah, they're pretty. But you know how sometimes that sort of looks whack? Like a mask?" She shuddered. "The eyes are wild."

I recalled my wedding day and how badly my face hurt at the end of the night. "It probably hurts to smile all day."

"Yeah," Lee said, "but that's the contest, right?"

She shook her head, like, *What a shame.*

I nodded in agreement.

"It shouldn't be," I said. "But if that's the game, and they play it, then they're exploiting for their own gain the same patriarchal framework that seeks to subjugate them."

"*What?*"

I ordered a Diet Coke.

While Lee was gone, I thought of the many serious feminist texts I'd lugged with me to America's Playground, a.k.a. Atlantic City, a.k.a. the birthplace of Miss America. I'd brought theoretical ruminations on pageantry in general, and historical accounts of Miss America, and was thinking about memoirs written by the winners themselves—including *How to Win a Beauty Contest*, by Miss America 1949, Jacque Mercer. Mercer's book includes chapters like "What to Do When You Win" and "How to Accept Applause" and "How to Smile When You Don't Want To."

She writes:

There is nothing more exciting to an audience member than to see a pretty girl smiling through her tears and saying something like, 'Oh, Mamma! I won! I won!' Of course, no beauty queen would go so far as to do the overhead clasp of a prize fighter in acknowledgment, but if people are nice enough to applaud, then you should be gracious and charming enough to bow and smile in return.

Mercer urges her readers to embrace "a few simple tricks that will help you smile more easily on all occasions"—tricks like:

"If you are walking down the street, make a game of smiling at lampposts or at every mailbox you see."

I was practicing smiling through the window at the parking lot when Lee returned with my drink.

"Another thing I forgot to say? They barely eat." She wiggled her head back and forth. "It's always 'egg whites, egg whites, egg whites.'"

I cracked my Diet Coke can and laughed, interpreting her impression of the girls as the performance of a more body-confident woman, one befuddled by dieting.

But Lee wasn't laughing.

"I wish I could be skinny," she whispered.

"You're perfect," I lied.

*   *   *

Atlantic City's Boardwalk Hall boasted 10,500 seats, but during the first night of preliminaries, only around seven people sat in each section. The auditorium was almost empty. The competition began with a third of the contestants parading onstage to the empowering sound of Rachel Platten's "Fight Song," chosen for the pageant by Nick Jonas, that year's official "music curator." After that, they disappeared, returning in bikinis for "Lifestyle and Fitness,"* which counted for 15 percent of their preliminary score.

Dena Blizzard, a Miss America loser turned comic (her one-woman show, *One Funny Mother: I'm Not Crazy!!*, premiered off-Broadway in April 2015), introduced the Lifestyle and Fitness competition in accordance with the organization's stance:

"First, it's a demonstration of athleticism and strength," she said, "an indicator of how hard the women work, a testament to health, a motivating counterexample, the first step toward a war on obesity."

Blizzard lifted her fist in solidarity and said:

"It's not about being a size two."

But then out marched the contestants, all of whom definitely looked like size 2s—except maybe for Miss Kentucky,

---

* The bikini part of the competition was officially banned in 2018.

whom the audience members in my midst jeered at, making fun of her face and her hopes and her dreams (she was eighteen and wanted to be president of the United States).

"Eighteen?" a middle-aged woman next to me hissed. "She looks forty-two!"

"President? More like First Lady," another said.

"More like fat ass."

They laughed.

I showed my teeth.

Behind us, a husky daughter stood up in front of her husky mom, swinging her hips in a pantomime of Miss Kentucky's walk and puffing out her cheeks, giggling, parroting the older women's mean insinuations about Miss Kentucky's weight.

"It's not about that," her mother admonished. "It's how she do."

Eveningwear came next and counted for 20 percent, then talent—a portion of the night that could easily be retitled "Who Is Most Like a Jane Austen Character?" Almost every contestant played a little instrument, or did an impressive short dance, or sang a nice song. Talent counted for 35 percent. (I learned that at some point, a private ten-minute interview had taken place and counted for 25 percent. But the organization didn't show us that part. Apparently the producers considered it too boring to witness girls in conversation.) Each contestant was granted sixty seconds to discuss her "platform," defined by the Miss America website as "an issue about which she cares deeply and that is of relevance to our country." This section of the evening was brief, incoherent (by virtue of the stopwatch), and ultimately very low stakes, counting for only 5 percent of each person's overall score.

As they announced that night's winners (during the preliminaries, participants won small trophies for looking good in swimsuits), I glanced behind me at the woman and her daughter to see how they'd take the news. Miss Kentucky had sashayed across the stage with the easy confidence of a future president. According to the mother's logic—"It's how she do"—she should have won the prize. But the judges didn't agree. Blizzard called South Carolina's name—the victor of that night's preliminaries—and all the size 2 losers hugged each other, evidently thrilled that another size 2 had beaten them. The mother handed her daughter earbuds and an iPad as a consolation prize.

"Show me that pretty smile," she said.

* * *

The bikini march was always controversial. But since its inception it had also been the lifeblood of the pageant.

In Miss America's early years, the bangable-body requirement was much more explicit and, in certain cases, defined with scientific specificity. When Norman Rockwell judged Miss

America in 1923, contestants were awarded up to 15 points for the "construction of their heads." Until 1935, judges unfurled measuring tapes to determine whether contestants possessed the ideal bust-waist-hip ratios. That same year, the Miss America Organization recruited Lenora Slaughter, formerly of the St. Petersburg, Florida, Chamber of Commerce, to become the head of the pageant. She instituted reforms designed to make the pageant more respectable, which meant forgoing the official cataloging of body proportions and changing the name of the "bathing suit" category to "swimwear," because she thought "bathing" conjured the idea of sex. She also banned women who were not "of good health and the white race" from competing, a fact that goes uncharted in the organization's renderings of her. Slaughter ran the pageant for more than thirty years and is basically responsible for creating what we think of today as Miss America. (Her whites-only rule was abolished in 1950.)

Based on all the mean things I heard people whisper when the girls were in their bathing suits, audience members seemed to blame contestants for the bikini portion of the contest, often implying that the girls did it for attention. This is silly when one considers that the Miss America hopefuls—physically perfect, young, and gorgeous—could simply cross the boardwalk to the beach and receive much more legible (i.e., lecherous) attention. It's hard to see anybody's jaw drop with the spotlights in your eyes.

But the idea that participants in beauty-centric circuits crave some sexual satisfaction from the circus isn't new. In Dr. David Reuben's bestselling 1969 book, *Everything You Always Wanted to Know About Sex* (*But Were Afraid to Ask)*, he argues that pageant contestants bare their bodies for sexual gratification. "They usually have trouble attaining orgasm and never find much real pleasure in genital sex," he explains. "They show off their breasts, hips, buttocks and a discreet outline of the vulva (through a bathing suit) to admiring men." Essentially, Reuben says, the swimwear portion of the event gives participants titillation they can't experience anywhere else because they are sexually dead inside. According to him, the vulvas they display are numb.

So it's strange that none of the former Miss Americas I talked to said anything about having an orgasm while walking in a bikini across a dangerously slick stage in five-inch heels, or while being crowned. Miss America 1998, Kate Shindle, author of the 2014 memoir *Being Miss America: Behind the Rhinestone Curtain*, told me girls have to psych themselves up for that portion of the evening by justifying it to themselves as an athletic event. "Many [of the girls] are frightened by having to walk down a runway in a swimsuit. Many perspire heavily, shake, gag, or even throw up," Frank Deford wrote in his 1971 book, *There She Is: The Life and Times of Miss America*, known to amateur pageant historians as the "Miss America Bible."

According to one of the many moms I spoke with in the elevators and restrooms of the Claridge, "Girls stumble, twist ankles—it's scary! My daughter goes into it very anxious. That stuff really hurts, and they see it hurt their friends."

She confided in me that one of the less reported and admittedly uncommon injuries occurs when the girls are trying to change out of their bikinis after Lifestyle and Fitness is over. Sometimes, if they've gotten a little overzealous with the butt glue, which is sprayed onto a contestant's cheeks to keep her bikini bottom from slipping into her butt, they wind up tearing off skin.*

During the brief moment that they were handed microphones and permitted to speak for sixty seconds, many of the girls that week discussed fitness. In keeping with the organization's stance, a good number of them had taken up some form of health-related issue as their platform.

Miss Georgia's was a group called Healthy Children, Strong America.

When asked to describe her commitment to the cause, she simply said, "I really try to live my platform and exercise all the time."

"What do you say about that butt?" a lady stranger asked, poking at my glossy program while Miss Georgia

---

* From their butts.

showcased her glistening, perfect body. She leaned over to turn my page, clutching her plastic cup, reeking of sticky-sweet juice and rum. I pictured a mailbox in place of her face and smiled at it.

"What butt?" I said.

"The black lady's butt."

"Miss South Carolina?" I said.

"It's huge." She turned abruptly to her boyfriend, or who-ever he was, for confirmation, splashing purple drink on my lap. But he'd fallen fast asleep.

It reminded me of a scene in Deford's 1971 book, where a female judge complains of the entire ranking process get-ting thrown off by male judges, because they aren't harsh enough—they don't notice the same flaws that women see in other women.

"The whole trouble with male judges," the judge told Deford, "is that they can look right at a fanny and not even see the fanny overhang."

"Hey!"

The drunk woman was back in my face, head lolling side to side. She jabbed again at my program, indicating Miss South Carolina.

"I guess it's pretty big, for a butt," I heard myself say.

In response, she told me I had pretty hair, which I thanked her for by saying something about Miss Kentucky's cellulite.

This was how we complimented each other, by denigrating the girls.*

Blizzard joked throughout the night about how this year's ninety-fifth anniversary of the pageant also marked the twentieth anniversary of the year she competed and lost. I could see the teleprompter from where I was sitting, so I knew she was straying constantly off script,** abruptly shifting from serious adulation for health and wellness to compulsively mentioning her age, holding out her microphone so that a girl could talk about her platform issue only to interrupt with some crack about the difference in their ages. She smiled the entire time, but after a while it started to look like a fear grin.

"She needs to take a page out of Vanessa Williams's book and straight-up disappear," someone joked.

Earlier that week, it had been announced that Miss America would welcome Vanessa Williams to the judges' booth for the finals competition, which was a huge deal. After Williams became the first black woman ever to win Miss America in 1983, someone leaked photos of her doing a soft-core girl-on-girl pussy-licking modeling shoot, and the Miss America

---

* I've tried and failed to call contestants of Miss America anything but "girls," mostly because that's what those closest to the pageant call them. "I don't think they mean it pejoratively," Kate Shindle (Miss America 1998) assured me over the phone. "That's always just been the casual term that was tossed around."

** "Sometimes I have things planned," Blizzard told the *Press of Atlantic City*, regarding her upcoming gig at Miss America. "Sometimes things just happen."

Organization forced her to resign. Even prior to the photos, Williams had been getting it from all sides: the diversity groups didn't think she was "black enough"; the white supremacists found out where she lived and sent strange powders to her mother's house. In the midst of public humiliation and censure, a weaker woman might have lain down under the boardwalk to be eaten by feral cats. Instead, Williams became famous for other things, like acting and doing that song, "Save the Best for Last," which everyone forgets they know all the words to until it comes on in the car.

As hours passed and more girls twirled batons onstage, the shit-talkers' heckling started to feel inclusive, even womanly. Not participating in the catty commentary felt somehow unfriendly. And there's nothing as ugly in a woman as unfriendliness.

One lady nudged me and pointed to the stage. "Nose job, right?"

I didn't know whether she meant the contestant had gotten a nose job or needed one. Regardless, I agreed.

"She needs a breast lift," someone muttered—and then, later, "Either she's got implants, or that's a padded bra."

Enhancements like padded bras—called "falsies" in the past—were absolutely prohibited in early pageants. In fact, beautifying subterfuge was so taboo that in 1938, Miss California was rumored to have been blackballed in the finals because she "used too much makeup for the satisfaction of the judges" (she got first runner-up).

But by now, the organization condoned what it used to condemn, choosing sponsors that would spray-tan the girls at no charge or provide them with free shaping swimwear. Padding, mascara, and hair extensions were all part of the game. As one of the maids who cleaned up after the contestants told me, "You go into their rooms, and it's hair extensions! So many! Lined up on the floor small to big, like a staircase of hair!"

Going into the preliminaries, I saw falsies as an act of empowerment that proved gender could be constructed. I agreed with the feminist scholar Susan Bordo, who said, "Although our cultural work as feminists can and should expose the oppressiveness of social institutions such as the Miss America Pageant system, the pleasure of participation, of decorating and shaping the body, can have subversive potential."

I personally owned padded bras. I'd even purchased the Kardashian-endorsed waist trainer, which allowed me to complement exquisitely contoured breasts with a 1950s cinched waist. My favorite shapers were a few thongs with reinforced crotches designed to obfuscate camel toe, made by the brand Camel No.

But in Atlantic City, my falsies felt hot and itchy and uncomfortable—and I wondered what Dr. David Reuben would say about all my special underwear and corsets—what he might claim that I actually wanted.

Instead of thinking too much about it, the next day I wriggled into a pair of Spanx with butt pads and returned to Boardwalk Hall for more Miss America. Every night, the audience stood to sing our national anthem. The American flag hanging on the rear wall of Boardwalk Hall was three times bigger than the jumbotrons hanging on either side of the stage—both of which were partially obscured by the overhead speakers so that during close-ups, the girls looked decapitated. It became harder and harder to see them as people.

Later that week I would decide to take a relaxing walk on the beach. I pried off my shoes and socks on the sandy wooden ramp leading to the shore. Sighing, I eased into the sand and promptly cut my foot on garbage.

Mangy cats skulked from underneath the causeway, apparently smelling my blood.

"Pussy above, pussy below!" a clever drunk man yelled, pointing between the Miss America posters decorating Board-walk Hall and a sign telling tourists not to feed the cats.

* * *

According to the top brass at the Miss America Organization, winners always go on to do great things.

In some cases, "great things" includes going to war.

Miss Utah 2007 and Miss Kansas 2013 both enlisted before competing in the pageant (neither won the Miss America title), but apparently contestants enlist after winning, too.

At first, I was surprised by how many veterans were mentioned among Dena Blizzard's shout-outs to former Miss Americas, if only because competing in the system required total subscription to traditional feminine beauty standards, with which helmets and camouflage and machine guns clashed.

Yet correlations between the beauty contest and war run deep. In her essay "I Was Miss Meridian 1985: Sororophobia, Kitsch, and Local Pageantry," Donelle Ruwe, PhD, argues that by learning to think of beauty as a series of movements, outfits, and gender-enhancing prosthetics, contestants learn, perhaps even faster and more clearly than students in a gender-theory class, that gender is a construct. Simply winning Miss America can be seen as an almost martial triumph—a sort of Trojan-horse maneuver, whereby the winner manipulates the system by mirroring the same forces that oppress her.

Like soldiers, contestants train for years in the hopes of deployment. Whoever wins Miss America wears her crown overseas to rally American troops, shedding her own identity to become someone for everyone. Deford refers to Miss America's year with the title as a "moral crusade" on behalf of the organization and to Miss America herself as a "War Cheerleader."

Even the bikini she wears to win her title is named for the Marshall Island of Bikini, where, during World War II, the United States secretly tested its atomic bomb.*

Natural beauty and poise are myths created by men. The truth is that, like martial arts, both take time to master. In an interview with Deford quoted in his book, Miss America 1948, BeBe Shopp, says of her win, "I just figured if you could learn to be a brain, you could learn to be a woman."

Becoming the perfect woman requires training; you learn to wave and smile and forget yourself—just so. Winning Miss America, like winning a war, requires an individual to adopt a specific competitive identity, often at the expense of her real one.

There's a part in Deford's book about Jacque Mercer (the Miss America winner who wrote a book about smiling at mailboxes) that reads:

> Each year as she grew up, her father had given Jacque a battery of standard personality tests. The development of her character was charted consistently, and in the year before she became Miss America, her indices of drive, ambition, and self-confidence

---

* By the time natives returned to Bikini more than forty years later, they recognized nothing of that home. They were forced to leave again not long after because of radiation in the food supply; the island is still considered uninhabitable.

had risen so high that they appeared to have soared off the curve. She took the same tests following her year as Miss America, and found that those three characteristics had been shattered. Her best had been broken.

Mercer won, and lost herself.

* * *

"How old are you?" the woman sitting next to me asked. We knew each other now, not by name, but because our tickets sat us together every night. (Embarrassed by the low audience turnout, the organization had started hustling tourists on the boardwalk with free tickets. It had become impossible to switch seats.)

"Thirty," I said proudly.

Since the age of twelve, I'd always rounded up. And if turning thirty was a socially constructed, antifeminist preoccupation, why should I be afraid to say I was thirty when I was actually slightly younger?

"You look older," the woman said.

I reminded myself that at twelve, I would have taken this as a compliment.

That night, rather than wander the boardwalk, with its feral cats and lurid strangers, I went straight to my hotel room, collapsed on the bed, and snow-angeled the covers, relieved that after the next day's Show Me Your Shoes Parade, I would attend the final night of competition, and then I could go home, where my husband lived. I missed him. A few weeks earlier, we'd gone to one of those restaurants that specialize in fresh seafood and has tanks full of live lobsters and crabs to prove it. One of the crabs was so huge and terrifying, we spent most of the night talking about how it belonged in the Museum of Natural History behind a plaque designating it as a monster. While we shit-talked, it started to crawl across the bodies of other crabs and shellfish, and we watched in stunned horror as it curled one bony arm over the lip of the tank and managed to raise its eyes (were those eyes?) about an inch out of the water.

It was trying to pull itself out of the tank.

I gripped my husband's hand, simultaneously hoping for and rooting against the crab's escape. It struggled for what felt like hours before losing its grip and falling backward onto the depressed lobsters below. I stood abruptly, but my husband pulled me back into my seat. "Don't you dare try to save it," he said. He knows me better than anyone.

Now, in my Claridge hotel room, I curled into a fetal position, imagining a crab version of the giant Atlantic City pretzels I'd been eating sliding its bready limbs under my skin. I took deep breaths, willing my metabolism to destroy the monster.

All night, I tried to remind myself that it wasn't feminist to feel fat.

*   *   *

The Miss America Organization describes the Show Me Your Shoes Parade as an opportunity for contestants to celebrate "the spirit of their home state through costume and one-of-a-kind wearable handmade art-shoe creations. Floats, marching bands, dancers, twirling groups, and a variety of other amazing parade groups will join the fun!"

That year's parade took place in the pouring rain. Marching bands and banner-draped convertibles crawled down the boardwalk to avoid skidding. Pageant contestants perched on the backseats waved and smiled and twisted one leg midair without rest, somehow managing to hold their toes at a perfect forty-five-degree angle to their faces the whole time. Luckily their makeup was waterproof.

All around me, people praised the girls for acting like they weren't cold. When little toddler pageant girls marched past with dead expressions—because when you're that young you smile when you're happy, and there's nothing happy about being cold and wet and wearing itchy sequins—the women in my midst tried to rile them up, shouting, "C'mon, girls! Get it!"

I remember one time when I was that age, standing in a poufy-sleeved Easter dress that I hated because it was lavender and I wanted to wear a tuxedo like my ventriloquist dummy. My dad was taking a photo and said, "Smile, pumpkin!" But as soon as he prompted me, I forgot how to do it. Trying to remember, I pictured a cartoon, the way the teeth line up on top of each other, and arranged my top and bottom teeth that way, widening my eyes. My dad looked horrified. "What are you doing?" he asked. He thought I was angry with him, lashing out. After that I learned how to do it right, smiling all the time so as not to upset people, and by high school I'd won myself a solid reputation for being stupid (people loved me!), and permanent nasolabial folds that made me resemble my talking puppet.

By the time Miss Virginia passed by, the rain was coming down so hard that my sneakers and socks were squelching, and I could feel my toes shriveling into frozen raisins. Virginia's curls were collapsing, but everyone cheered because she pretended it wasn't happening. I went to a place in my head that was warm, like Virginia in July.

The sound of booing interrupted my reverie.

I looked up and saw a car approaching with its retractable top cranked up against the rain. Miss Wisconsin, from my home state, passed by us, guarded from the downpour, trying to hold her foot up to the passenger-side window to show us her shoes. She waved at us from behind the glass. People booed louder and louder.

"Now, that's just ridiculous," the woman shouted from under her golf umbrella. "We're out here in the rain, aren't we?"

"Poor sportsmanship."

"Not even trying."

"Did you see her frown?"

But she looks so cramped and uncomfortable, I wanted to say. *Isn't that enough?*

Instead, I booed.

I was the loudest of them all.

* * *

People love to boo at Miss America. A few years ago on *Last Week Tonight*, the cartoonishly incredulous John Oliver and a team of fact-checkers went after the Miss America Organization's 2014 claim that it had made $45 million available in academic scholarships. As a registered nonprofit, Miss America has to file public tax forms, so Oliver and the fact-checkers dug those up from 2012 and found that they showed an annual national scholarship expenditure of only $482,000. "A mere forty-four and a half *million* dollars short!" Oliver chortled to the camera, nearly choking on his own alarm.

I'm not sure if the Miss America Organization saw Oliver's bit, but the next year's official program quoted only $303,000 in scholarships. Perhaps the higher-ups were trying to deflect attention from recent rumors, based on other tax returns, that its current executive director, Sam Haskell III—a pink, sticky-looking man—had paid himself twice, as a boss and an employee, making away with hundreds of thousands of Miss America dollars over several years.

Ultimately, John Oliver and his team were depressed to find that the organization's biggest claim to fame—that it was the number one provider of scholarships to women in the world—was actually true.

Say what you will about Miss America. But as of 2015 it was one of a tiny number of organizations awarding smart, talented, hardworking ladies the lump sum of money needed for college.

*   *   *

"She looked fat in those photos," someone remarked as we waited in the dark for the finals to start.

She was talking about Vanessa Williams, around whom a new scandal was swirling. According to TMZ, there was some kind of mix-up about her coming back. Williams's people had expected her to receive a public apology, on live television, from the Miss America Organization, which had historically shunned nonwhite people, and had slut-shamed Williams in front of the entire nation. But the Miss America Organization believed that Williams was the one who would be apologizing to them.

Anyway, by the time the hosts charged onstage, waving at no one, and announced Williams's entrance, all of that unpleasantness seemed to have been resolved—because then there she was, Miss America 1983, floating onstage in a fabulous, iridescent toga. After she finished singing her song, Miss America director Sam Haskell III entered. He wrapped his arm around Williams's waist, held the microphone to his wormy lips, and smiled.

She smiled back at him, presumably picturing a mailbox.

"Though none of us currently involved in the organization were involved then," he began, already reneging all responsibility, "on behalf of today's organization, I want to apologize." A few people clapped. "To you, and to your mother, Miss Helen Williams, I want to apologize for anything that was said or done that made you feel any less the Miss America you are and the Miss America you always will be!"

Then Haskell and Williams did something crazy—in front of everyone, they told each other, "I love you."

The only thing I could think of was that maybe it was code. In his book Deford writes that Miss Americas win based on poise—a sort of indescribable attribute that he explains like this: "When a judge says that he has found *a girl with poise*, all the others realize that . . . it means: 'I love you.'" So in this case, maybe by telling each other "I love you," Haskell and

Williams were staging a truce—saying, "We're both winners here," or something?

But in reality there would only be one winner. An hour later, Miss America (formerly Miss Georgia) staggered gracefully down the runway in her crown, and the camera cut to Williams. Her expression was so fierce and steady it elicited whispers from those huddled around me about whether she'd had too much Botox. Her still and stony face seemed to say, *Under my rictus of congratulations, I have nothing but pity for you, Miss America*—but before I could consider it too deeply, I felt an internal swelling that, at first, I thought might be the pretzels coming up, but then I recognized it: *love.*

I loved the new Miss America. As she sobbed, I nodded soulfully, witheringly, satisfied with her delicate reaction— because by then I knew by heart that it was only proper to win modestly, and that it was up to me to judge. And although some instinctive part of me wanted to blame Vanessa Williams for her unwillingness and/or physiological inability to smile, I forgave her, too, because that's the ladylike thing to do. I smiled for both of us, knowing it was my job as a woman to feign happiness.

It wasn't the first time that week I had felt love. A few days prior, I had been grinning through pain. Some combination of salty sea air and nonbreathable body shapers had conspired to give me a full-blown bladder infection. On my way back from the CVS downtown with my Cipro tablets and Uricalm Max, I decided that giant cotton underpants were more practical than synthetic vagina hammocks and detoured to the outlet mall, trudging zombielike in the wake of flocks of scooter-riding tourists to wait in line for granny panties. Just then my symptoms kicked in again. I had the sudden, unstoppable urge to pee, threw my grown-up undies on the floor, and scrambled to one of the public toilets at the Atlantic City Greyhound bus terminal, the refuge of the desperate.

While I winced on the toilet, a child's foot slid under the stall divider, brushing my ankle. I assumed some little girl was trying to peek at me. But then the child's calf slid into my stall, and then the rest of the leg, and the head—and it wasn't a little kid at all, but a petite young woman with neck tattoos and the plunger of an empty heroin needle clenched between her teeth, melting into my stall. She had tied off with a cell phone charging cord, the same one I had in my purse.

By the sinks, the women who parked their scooters in the hall now murmured to one another, voices slowly rising for someone—"anyone!"—to call the cops.

I pulled up my shorts a little too soon, peeing on myself, and got down on my knees to shake her, dragging her into my stall and thinking, "Her arms are so soft."

A man shouted from the doorway, "Hey, Cricket, come on, you're going to get arrested."

Cricket's eyes rolled open. Her color looked good. She hadn't overdosed, I thought. She was just very, very high—not that I knew anything at all. I just watched a lot of TV.

As police sirens wailed in the distance, I thought about how hard it is to sneak up on an actual cricket. They have ears in their legs, and their tympanal organs make them extremely sensitive to vibrations. But this Cricket had no awareness of my presence. I leaned her against the partition and untied her cell phone cord without eliciting any reaction. I wondered what her talent was—everybody has one. A melody or dance seemed likely. Of all the singing insects, scientists agree that crickets are the most musically gifted. They keep a wide variety of songs in their toolbox, each with its own individual purpose: mating, rivalry, a new relationship. Their chirping is thought to bring good luck.

"Ugh," Cricket said, her blue eyes rolling open. They were gorgeous, like the sea.

The cops were yelling now, warning ladies to get out, they were coming in. I wriggled the syringe out of Cricket's mouth and slipped it into my back pocket, thinking that maybe if she didn't have it on her, she wouldn't go to jail. I stuffed the cell phone cord in her purse. I tried to lift her, but she was heavier than she looked, and she slid back down.

Walkie-talkies crackled. The cops were banging on my stall.

"Come out," they shouted.

I let them in.

"I think she's just drunk," I lied. "Wait—I think I know her."

But they were pushing me away. They could tell by my clean hair and my shopping bag that I had nothing to do with it. I wasn't a beauty, but I wasn't a junkie, either. Each of us has her place.

Outside, I tossed the bloody needle in a trash can and walked to the Taj Mahal, remembering my husband and the crab: "Don't you dare try to save it."

The truth is I wouldn't even have touched her if she hadn't been so beautiful.

Snowflake

A lot of things caused Susie pain: scented products, pesticides, plastic, synthetic fabrics, smoke, electronic radiation—the list was long. Back in the "regular world," car exhaust made her feel sick for days. Perfume gave her seizures.

Then she uprooted to Snowflake, Arizona.

"I got out of the car and didn't need my oxygen tank," she said, grinning at me in the rearview mirror. "I could walk."

There were about twenty households where she now lived. Like Susie, most of the residents in Snowflake had what they called "environmental illness," a controversial diagnosis that attributed otherwise unexplained symptoms to pollution.

My knees knocked together as she swerved onto another dirt road. Mae, a filmmaker, was busy shooting scenery from the front seat. We'd come for four days to find out why dozens of people chose to make their homes here, and Susie had agreed to host us only if we did not seek outside opinion from psychiatrists regarding their condition. "He's got it bad," she said, nodding at a neighbor's driveway. The sign out front read: NO UNINVITEDS.

My eyes darted over barbed wire cattle fences and dead juniper trees. White mountains swam in the distance. We stopped, and Susie motioned for Mae to open a gate decorated in yellow Christmas tinsel. A shadowy figure stood at the top of the gravel drive, surrounded by shrubs and sand and nothing.

*   *   *

The idea that modern conveniences cause pain dates to the mid-nineteenth century. In 1869, Dr. George Beard published several papers blaming modern civilization and steam power for ailments such as "drowsiness, cerebral irritation, pain, pressure and heaviness in the head."

According to him, other indications of chemical sensitivity included "fear of society, fear of being alone, fear of contamination . . . fear of fears . . . fear of everything."

Beard called the illness "neurasthenia." Susie called it being "sensitive to the whole world."

Susie had warned us that Deb, a sort of roommate who lived in her driveway, was extremely sensitive to scents. In order to protect her, Mae and I had agreed to various terms: we would not get a rental car or stay at a motel, because those were places where chemical cleaners were used. We would wear Susie's clothes and sleep at Susie's house. She also made us swear not to get any perms before we came, which made me think she had been in the desert for a long time.

For weeks, Mae and I avoided makeup, lotion, perfume, hair products, scented detergent, fabric softener, dryer sheets.

We used fragrance-free soap and shampoo, as well as a natural deodorant, which, according to the description on the box, was basically a rock picked off the ground with a cap on it.

Despite our best efforts, Deb's sensitive nose picked up on chemical exhaust, which she said was "off-gassing" from our pores. For her, we reeked like a Bath & Body Works store flooded with vodka—or, as she put it, "floral, with chemical solvents."

"You're fragrant," she said.

Mae and I exchanged nervous glances, worried, based on Deb's expression, that they'd send us packing. Snowflake was not easy to get to. I'd risen at dawn, vomited on a tiny six-passenger plane, and walked one mile down a busy highway in a town called Show Low (160 miles from Phoenix) to get to Susie's car.

"We'll do our best to get you cleaned," Susie promised us. "I got lots of hydrogen peroxide."

It was decided that the best way to get us straight from the car into the shower, where we could wash the outside world's chemicals away, was to enter the house completely naked. So Mae and I took off our clothes and marched without dignity across the gravel driveway. We had known each other for about an hour.

"You can have the first shower," she said, wrapping herself in a towel.

"Thank you, Fay," I said.

"It's Mae," she said.

Susie's bathroom, like the rest of her one-room, off-grid house, was wallpapered in heavy-duty Reynolds Wrap. Above the toilet, a small, sealed window looked out at the desert. I saw a gnarled juniper tree and a wild hare scampering into a hole that Susie had said contained a nest of baby rabbits. I scrubbed off with a bar of olive oil soap and inhaled the metallic scent of hard water. It was the only thing I could smell.

Someone knocked. Mae reluctantly asked if I wore underwear. "We're playing dress-up!" Susie shouted from the other room.

I realized what Mae actually meant was *Did I wear Susie's underwear?* I hesitated for a moment, considering the alternative: going commando in a sandy environment.

"Hey, Kathleen!" Susie yelled. "Do you—"

"I wear underwear," I called.

Later, we gathered in the kitchen. Deb was sensitive to grains, GMO foods, preservatives, and all artificial flavoring and coloring, so we ate cabbage soup for dinner. I foresaw a painful night of off-gassing.

Afterward, Mae and I ducked behind a curtained-off partition to consider our sleeping arrangements: two metal cots, one broken, and zero blankets (because blankets were absorbent and, according to local logic, our pores might still be off-gassing dangerous chemicals). Nighttime in the desert is freezing, and Susie's house did not have heating, because heating was poison. I wanted badly to be unconscious and regretted my semi-recent decision to start weaning off sedatives.

Asked whether she might at least have some padding to cover the iron springs, Susie retreated outside, shouting over her shoulder, "FYI, the rats here are aggressive." She returned with dirt-caked bathmats, which smelled strongly of urine, and I imagined that Susie's territorial dog, who was asleep at the time with his eyes open, was probably the culprit, although I could also imagine a family of aggressive rats peeing on the rugs in some kind of vindictive jamboree.

"There," she said, turning off the lights. "Comfy."

That night Mae and I, basically complete strangers, climbed into the same cot to stay warm. I tried to be professional about my role as big spoon. But eventually I removed the modesty towel that I had stuffed between my crotch bone and her tailbone. We needed it as a blanket, and full body contact, with the minimal warmth that provided, seemed like the only route to sleep. I'd never experienced such extended cold. And I grew up in Wisconsin, a place so freezing I once saw a drunk boy start to cry in the middle of publicly urinating.

"I'm putting my arm around you," I said to Mae. "I was trying to be professional before by keeping it pinned to my side, but it's been numb for an hour now and I worry if I don't cuddle you it might have to be amputated."

"You don't have to use the verb 'cuddle,'" Mae pointed out. "Just do it and we don't have to talk about it anymore."

We huddled in wretched silence. Susie's voice echoed in my head.

"Etiquette is: you defer to whoever's the sickest in any household," she had said in the car, but at the time, I hadn't recognized it as a warning.

I reminded myself that whatever discomfort we felt paled in comparison to how she and Deb had suffered in the regular world.

*   *   *

Susie grew up in forested Northern California and spent most of the 1970s in the Bay Area, working odd jobs and traveling with her boyfriend. As friends started dropping like flies from an illness nobody could understand, Susie endured respiratory, gastrointestinal, and neurological symptoms. It hurt her feelings when doctors suggested she might just have anxiety.

While the AIDS epidemic kicked into crisis mode, Susie's symptoms got worse, intensifying whenever she smelled smoke or saw power lines. Unable to function, she moved back home, where, through an autodidactic game of trial and error, she identified what triggered her worst symptoms. She slept on her parents' porch or on the bathroom floor, because those were the only places she could breathe. Her mother collected rain for her to drink.

Now using a wheelchair, she returned to San Francisco to pursue a master's degree in disability policy. She launched the *Reactor*, an environmental illness advocacy newsletter, which circulated via an underground network of hypersensitive people throughout the country. An environmentally ill reader told Susie the air where he lived was "clean enough for him to manage," and in 1994, Susie followed him to Snowflake, where the tiny community (only a handful of people at the time) immediately rallied around her. Within a year, her father and neighbors pooled their resources to build her a house—"a little, safe place."

Meanwhile, across the country, her future roommate Deb's life had never felt more dangerous.

* * *

Like Susie, Deb's initial thought was AIDS. After ruling that out, she juggled endless skepticism. Even those who believed she felt ill wrote it off, saying she'd bounce back.

Deb had always been strong. As a child living on Lake Michigan, she sailed and played sports. After attending Michigan Technological University and getting married, she worked for nine years as the only female metallurgical engineer at Bendix aircraft; her specialty was failure analysis.

When she became pregnant, Deb kept working with metals, inhaling zinc and cadmium—nobody told her not to—but all she could smell was her coworkers' cologne and aftershave. Scented products sent her body into crisis. She vomited a lot.

After giving birth in 1992, Deb left work to parent full-time. She lived in a moldy house with a smoky furnace. Infections blowtorched her sinuses, turning into migraines that hit her like an ax. Her weight plummeted to seventy-five pounds. Doctors said she was anorexic.

Finally, Deb couldn't take it anymore. She left Michigan when her daughter was sixteen and became itinerant, sleeping in her truck, because unlike plastic or drywall, metal emitted no chemical fumes and was safe.

The same word-of-mouth network that beckoned Susie eventually led Deb to Snowflake, where she performed chores for the environmentally sick in exchange for food. By the time Susie spotted her out boiling clothes for a neighbor, Deb had been living in her truck for five years and needed a place to park. The two women became a domestic duo. Deb cooked "clean food" for Susie on the hot plate. They made each other laugh and protected each other. Susie remained compassionately straight-faced when Deb finally admitted she hadn't seen her daughter in seven years.

By the age of sixty-seven, Susie had finally put her master's degree to use, although not in the way she had originally intended. She had become Snowflake's unofficial welcome wagon, local therapist, and advocate. She sat with men and women who were sick with something no one else believed in, and she believed them. She fielded at least five long phone calls a night from the bedridden and lonely, talking to them for as long as they needed company. She helped people with the arduous paperwork involved in collecting government aid. She reassured them that their illness wouldn't kill them—it would only "hurt, a lot."

Everyone whom Mae and I met loved her and got tears in their eyes when they said so.

* * *

Historically speaking, settlers' reasons for uprooting typically established the hierarchy wherever they resettled. Puritans relocated for religious reasons, so the devout became leaders. Forty-niners rushed in search of gold, and those who struck it gained status.

But people came to Snowflake to nurture disease, so here, illness acted like a social currency. Being "normies"—a mostly derogative term meaning that chemical fragrances and electricity didn't (yet) cause us debilitating pain—not only dropped Mae and me into a category of people who had historically hurt, abandoned, and misdiagnosed everyone we were about to meet; it also ranked us as lepers.

139

Luckily, I was about to become very sick.

On day two, I woke with a crick in my neck, a headache, a creeping sense of self-hatred, and Mae's hair in my mouth.

"Did you sleep?" she said.

I hadn't made any noise or moved beyond opening my eyes, but apparently we were at the point where we could sense each other's biorhythms.

"Yeah, did you?"

"I don't know," she said. The coils shrieked as she got off the cot. "I need to find coffee. I feel crazy."

"We can't tap out," I called after her. "I watch a lot of those reality television shows where people are, like, dropped naked and stuff on islands and told to survive, and I always tell myself I would never tap out on the first day."

I heard Susie's and Deb's voices in the other room and threw an elbow over my eyes, willing myself to cheer up. Despite my pep talk, I felt very close to tapping out. The headache I'd woken up with had snowballed into nausea. I was starting to feel the familiar, flu-like symptoms that for me pave the way for emotional darkness.

I had begged to write about Snowflake because I iden-tified with the idea of sick people retreating to the middle of nowhere to find peace. Almost two years earlier, I'd suffered a mental breakdown and retreated to a psychiatric hospital for two weeks. Medication and therapy had brought me back to reality. But I felt I recognized the urge to leave everything behind.

In the almost two years since my collapse, sticking to the to-do list they gave us at the psychiatric hospital (sleep; eat; take medication) had, at the very least, made me feel in control.

Now, each item had been compromised thanks to our sleeping arrangements, the unsatisfying house staple (cabbage), and my personal desire to, at some point, become pregnant with a baby that did not resemble an octopus.

"I'm starting to think now might not have been the best time to start tapering off psychotropic drugs," I said to Mae, who barely heard me.

"There's a situation," she replied.

In the kitchen, Susie and Deb revealed that trust issues had developed between us. The night before, Mae and I decided to charge her camera battery, and apparently it had kept Susie awake.

"But we could hear her snoring," I said.

"You hurt her," Deb said.

They wanted to know how they could be sure that we weren't just another pair of journalists here to play games—to test their disease with shenanigans and make fun of them.

Deb said we couldn't fool her.

As proof, she relayed a story about how, once, when her daughter was "ten or twelve," they'd gone together to the grocery store.

"I lost track of her and her friend," Deb said, smirking proudly, "and then I found them, and I could smell it. They claimed, 'No, no, no,' but I knew they'd gone and done perfume samples. So we're in the car, and they're giggling to themselves, and I told them to get out."

That was the end of the story.

"Did you make them get out of the car?" I said.

"Well, yeah," she said, looking confused. "We were only about three miles from home." She told me she turned the car around "eventually." But I couldn't help seeing it from the daughter's point of view: a friend had come over, and they'd been left on the highway.

I worried we were about to get kicked out, too.

I followed Deb's gaze to the window. Outside, Susie's dog had his nose in the nest of baby rabbits. His neck muscles jerked as he swallowed one whole.

"Nature is just awful," Deb said.

She and I went outside to pick up some of the blind, still-squirming litter with shovels. I thought we should smash their heads with the shovels and put them out of their misery, but Deb said we should return them to the nest, in case the mother returned and could save some of them. I watched as she put the living and dead back into the hole and covered it with a piece of metal, leaving a pocket for the mom to burrow through if she returned. Somehow I knew she wouldn't.

When we went back inside, the emotional meeting was called back into order. But I was distracted by the sight of Susie's dog reapproaching the nest. He started digging.

Deb said, in order to trust us going forward, we had to promise we weren't going to write anything but a positive piece that would clearly inform readers of the clinical validity of environmental illness.

"We can't promise that," Mae said.

A general silence fell over the aluminum foil room. Deb, who had been pretty emotionless up until then, looked like she might cry. Our chance at writing a story seemed to be disintegrating. So I cleared my throat and prepared to overshare in order to hopefully defuse things.

"I'll tell you a secret," I said.

*   *   *

I told Susie and Deb that I knew how it felt, at least a little bit, "to be sick and have nobody believe you." I explained how, four or five years earlier, my hair had started falling out, and I had had this awful burning sensation on the back of my scalp that was so intense I used a bag of ice as a pillow, and I had felt nauseated all the time, and tired, and cried a lot.

They softened. When I got to the part about how every other doctor I saw that year said I was fine, physically speaking, and had referred me to a psychiatrist, they scoffed knowingly and protectively. They asked what my environment had been like; I thought they meant emotionally, so I told them how I moved to New York for this guy, and we signed a lease together, broke up after one month—then I lost my job and had no savings—la-la-la.

Susie cut me short: "No, your physical environment."

I remembered, with a lurch, that our apartment had been downwind from a dry cleaner's. I used to go stand next to its vents because the detergent smelled great compared to the chicken slaughter plant down the street.

Susie and Deb looked like they wanted to high-five. To them, my proximity to harsh chemicals proved that my depression had been a symptom of environmental illness.

"They use all sorts of chemical agents to clean slaughterhouses," Deb said excitedly. "When you left, did the symptoms go away?"

"No, but they started to, a little, when this doctor friend of mine said to try eliminating gluten."

"The gluten, that's what happened with me!" Susie said. "That's one of the things I found I was sensitive to. It's commoner than people think."

"For me, personally, it was a placebo," I said carefully, clocking their disappointed looks. They cringed even more when I used the word "psychosomatic."

"The gluten-free thing helped for a long time, especially with the problem I'd had shitting my pants—I think just controlling my environment probably helped. But the scalp burning didn't go away until a dermatologist prescribed me antidepressants."

"That's not me saying the symptoms weren't real," I continued—and in my nervousness that I'd once again offended them, I then farted so shrilly that Mae laughed in shock.

Susie just shrugged and Deb remained completely impassive, as if maybe she hadn't heard, which was not possible. Chemicals bothered them, but bodily functions were fine.

Given the progress made by discussing my medical history, I publicized my current headache. Susie scrambled to get me Tylenol (apparently over-the-counter pain relief wasn't toxic), and Deb graciously explained that this was yet another sign my body was dumping toxins from the regular world. My illness had immediately elevated my status in the household. "Here you go," Deb said, handing me a mug. Susie tapped two pills into my palm.

After almost twenty-four hours of being told I stank and generally being treated like a contagious freak, I was so grateful for these ministrations that I went to hug them. Susie acquiesced, but Deb said I was still too fragrant for us to embrace.

"But I changed my mind," she said to Mae. "I'll let you film me, if you want."

* * *

Susie and Deb, like most of their neighbors, received disability checks. But welfare had not made them complacent. It wasn't easy to apply for disability when you suffered from an illness that most refused to recognize. And even if you did receive some aid, the checks could stop at any moment. All it took was one Arizona bureaucrat looking at your file and deciding that your sickness was made up. Or "psychosomatic."

Over and over again, residents emphasized to me that they wanted to work, they missed working—they had no identity now, they said, no sense of self-worth. Many, like Deb, were former chemical engineers. They were smart, easily bored, and embarrassed by what they worried some might misconstrue as laziness or mooching. I believed them when they said they wanted jobs. I also believed that they were far too sick to work. Many spent entire days in bed, eyes clenched against the blinding pain caused by their illness.

"People here suicide themselves," Susie said, as we trudged around the desert, collecting stones for her collection. She estimated that it happened around twice a year, which, given the shifting population of forty or so people, I pointed out, was an epidemic. Our boots crunched on petrified rabbit shit, twisted sticks, and rocks that were sometimes fossils—only Susie had said we couldn't call them fossils, because many of the people here were Christian and didn't believe in evolution. Sound carried so well that the hummingbirds overhead sounded like helicopters. Susie told us about a friend with environmental illness who had killed himself a few months prior.

"He wasn't depressed or anything; he just couldn't take it anymore, so he starved himself," she said. "We bury our own dead."

"I'm so sorry," I said.

Many of the people we met had finally found doctors who believed them. In the regular world, after enduring years of humiliating checkups and stints in the emergency room, they had relegated the medical profession to enemy status. Now, they spoke adoringly of their physicians, most of whom practiced integrative health—a blend of Western science, holistic healing, and one-on-one therapy.

As long as I framed environmental illness as a physical phenomenon, Snowflakers were happy, even eager, to communicate. But they got angry if I broached their illness, even obliquely, as a psychological phenomenon. They had spent years feeling sick and battling skeptics.

Later, breathing through another stomachache, I scanned my notes, rereading scrawled concerns based on various conversations about the potential that everyone we met had some form of extreme PTSD, either from being sick, witnessing a nationwide health crisis, or—as had cropped up in one or two of the conversations—from being sexually assaulted. I worried that if Mae and I represented this environmentally ill community in any fashion that wasn't simply a public service announcement about the validity of environmental illness, they might suicide themselves. I wasn't convinced that our chemical odors would kill Snowflake's residents. But our narrative about them might.

"Do you think it's real?" Mae asked. "The allergies? The pain?"

I nodded.

I showed her how, if you covered up the "environ" in "environmental illness," it spelled what I had.

* * *

At first, when I asked Susie whether she took any medications for her environmental illness, she cackled like a little girl and said, "None of your business!"

"I do, though," she continued after a pause. "For seizures."

Certain psychiatric drugs double as anti-seizure medications, so I rattled off a few familiar brand names. Susie nodded at one I took. I wondered if we had the same thing, whatever it was.

Later that day, my stomach cramps intensified. I wasn't supposed to get my period for two more weeks, so I hadn't brought tampons. Soon I was forced to make an uncomfortable announcement.

"Susie," I said, "I menstruated in your pants."

To my surprise, she was totally unfazed. Using her power outlets might have angered Susie, but when it came to the body's natural processes, she was patient and kind. "Take as many as you want," she said, unloading an armful of clean underwear into my lap. "Layer up! I wish we had something else for you."

Mae, anticipating a night of sharing a bed with me, quietly asked how heavy my flow was.

"Do you want a sock?" Deb asked, and reassured me endlessly that, yes, it was fine to use one of her socks as a maxi pad. She told me the only thing to worry about was that it was dark outside, and animals might smell my blood.

* * *

On our last morning in town, Deb intercepted me in the driveway to explain how fragile I was. She had been thinking about my symptoms—the headache, my history of so-called depression, and my menstrual cycle, which started two weeks early on our second day there.

"My therapist says it's just stress," I said.

I told her I thought we recognized something in each other, but chose to call it different things.

She shook her head. "You have environmental illness, I can sense it."

In a quiet, tentative voice, she explained to me that there was, in fact, an objective, scientific way to test me for environmental illness; she could do it right then and there. The procedure would be relatively painless, but I couldn't mention the specifics in my piece.

"I feel like this will sound more ominous than it is if I leave out the details," I said as we went through with the procedure.

"People will think we're crazy," she said.

"I am crazy," I said.

"No," she said.

After we finished, I lingered in the doorway while Deb searched the dark house for her glasses. I was no longer permitted indoors because I had changed back into my own clothes, and the scents emanating from my regular-world apparel had already caused Deb's ears to swell, making it hard for her to hear. It was time to go, but Deb said the apparatus she used to diagnose environmental illness wasn't working, so she would have to be in touch. I wrote down my phone number.

"Can I give you a hug good-bye?" I said.

"Not in those clothes," she said.

As Susie ferried us back into society, beef cattle glared at us from the ditches, and calves stumbled in the road. Susie told us she didn't see any overlap between mental and environmental illness. Certain substances were physically poisonous, and that was the end of it.

"If someone is reckless or careless about exposures that will cause issues for you, that is, to some measure, assaultive," Susie said.

"'Assault,' that's a strong word," Mae said.

"Yep," Susie said. "That's why I say it." She added, "You can be beat chemically, just like you can be beat with a fist."

"Susie, have you ever gotten beat with a fist?" I asked.

She turned to smile at me. "That's part of being female," she said. "But if someone has cancer, you don't say it's because they got hit as a kid."

*　　*　　*

At the airport gate, I remembered the emergency Valium in my bag, and all of my stress went away. But it wore off on the flight, and by the time I got home, I felt the sadness in my blood. I almost hoped Deb's test would work—that she would find something scientific to substantiate how shitty I sometimes felt.

A few days later, when they called me, Deb and Susie put me on speakerphone, because holding the receiver to their heads triggered neurological problems. Once again, they wanted me to tell them exactly what I would write about them. They worried I might make fun of them. I told them that wasn't my intention, but that I tended to tell the truth, at which point Deb told me that my test results had shown her that I was sick.

"But I can help you."

"We can help you shave off a couple years of fruitless effort," Susie added.

"What's wrong with me?" I said.

Deb promised she would tell me, eventually. But only after she read this piece.

"Isn't that, like, blackmail?" I said.

Susie and Deb started to laugh, softly and shrewdly.

I'm still waiting for my results.

First I Got Pregnant.
Then I Decided to
Kill the Mountain Lion.

In 2012, a mountain lion fled his home in the Santa Monica Mountains and journeyed twenty miles to Mount Hollywood. He slunk across freeways, bounding between trucks and across parking lots and through residents' front yards, all the way to the hills surrounding the iconic Hollywood sign, where he hid himself, right there among the public hiking trails.

During the day, he slept, occasionally snapping awake at the chatter of hikers. Below him stretched downtown Los Angeles, the Pacific Ocean, car exhaust billowing over crowded highways. After dusk, when the park closed and the spotlights at Paramount Studios danced across the polluted sky, he emerged from his nest to hunt, craving deer but settling for rats, which nested in the garbage cans near the public toilets.

Scientists suspected that the mountain lion had fled from the coast because things were getting crazy there. Resources were dwindling. One UCLA reporter wrote of "rivalry, slaughter, and incest." The Santa Monica Mountains were played out. Griffith Park, although comparatively tiny, seemed to suit him better. He spent his new life in solitude. A ghost cat.

But trail cameras eventually captured his presence, prompting Hollywood residents to panic in true Hollywood fashion. The park was a popular place for families. Its trails wove around the Hollywood sign and to the Griffith Observatory, where *Rebel Without a Cause* and *La La Land* had been filmed.

The park service issued reassurances that mountain lions (also called cougars or pumas) are basically shy creatures. To keep an eye on things, they sedated the animal, put a monitoring collar on him, named him P-22 (*P* for "Puma," *22* to indicate the number of urban mountain lions being tracked at the time), and released him back into the park.

During this time, I lived in New York City, unaware of P-22 and his Hollywood haunting.

Four years later, I had decided I would have to hunt and kill him.

* * *

Brooklyn had been broody and dark and angry in a way I'd loved. There, I drank too much in cozy booths, felt anonymous in crowds, got into mutually therapeutic swearing matches with strangers on the subway, waved my hands a lot while talking about books, and struggled to keep houseplants alive in our dim home.

In Los Angeles, our apartment boasted views of palm trees from the toilet and so much natural sunlight that you had to wear sunblock in the kitchen. On clear days, from our living room, you could see the Hollywood sign through the fog. Outside, people smiled. My husband and I made new friends who boasted of their sobriety and invited me on hikes. In spite of my long-honed East Coast cynicism, the paved desert entranced me. It felt healthy, the sort of place where a modern-day Jane Austen character might go to "take the cure." Evolutionary forces tied to environmental pleasures and age and general happiness elbowed my husband and me to reproduce. Our beatific surroundings sparked a roosting impulse.

Once the bliss of my first positive pregnancy test wore off, an animal panic set in. In order to exorcise from my mind the statistics surrounding miscarriage and genetic abnormalities, I gave up coffee, threw away my most effective acne creams, and ate organic, choking down unpalatable but nutrient-dense foods. Despite the West Coast diet, East Coast neuroticism clawed its way back into my brain. At 11:11, I kissed my fingers, muttering, "Strong baby." I spent several hours each day googling "make healthy fetus no problems how do I."

Since I had wanted to become pregnant, and even sort of planned for it, some of what I read online felt familiar. I'd already gone off the psychiatric drugs that might otherwise have given my fetus issues ranging from emotional problems to a micropenis, and I knew that I needed to take prenatal vitamins and avoid snorting cocaine. But other stuff surprised me, like apparently no one was allowed to rub the spot between my ankle bone and heel or I might go into premature labor, and I had to use plant-based beauty products, whatever those were, and the European studies about wine being okay were a myth, people over there were simply alcoholics, and if I bought baby clothes with buttons on them, the kid, if it survived gestation, would choke and die, and Tylenol, which I'd thought was fine, caused ADHD. I internalized it all.

Then one day I found myself struck by a pregnancy symptom euphemistically described by doctors as "breast tenderness," which felt like someone had cut off my nipples with a serrated knife. I tried ice and Vaseline, but when the pain would not break, I broke and swallowed two Tylenol.

Afterward, I called my best friend Sarah McKetta, now in medical school, and murmured that I'd just given my fetus a learning disability.

"Nah," she said. "It's all heredity and chance. Doctors can't say that to patients just in case something goes wrong and they sue for malpractice. But the truth is you can't mess this up."

She paused.

"Unless you binge drink every day or accidentally ingest abortion herbs. But I'm pretty sure they only sell those in Mexico."

She meant to reassure me—to remind me that entire cultures eat raw fish or drink wine while pregnant and carry on. "Think of our grandmothers," she said, and I knew exactly what she meant. Mine smoked and drank martinis throughout her seven healthy pregnancies, and they're all mostly high-functioning adults who've never had cancer. (When Nana found herself pregnant with my dad, her fourth child, her 1950s doctor—apparently horrified by Nana's admission that she felt fatigued and stressed out by being pregnant while tending to three children under the age of four—prescribed her amphetamines. Lots. And arguably my father's only defects are restless leg syndrome and being twice divorced.)

All of this suggested that if I miscarried or produced an imperfect child, it might not be the result of my pregnancy regimen. The argument was tailored to relieve me, but it did the opposite, because if I couldn't do anything to destroy my good fortune, then I couldn't do anything to protect it, either.

* * *

A few days after this realization, Trump was elected president, and at my next doctor's appointment, I found out we'd be having a girl. My husband made me promise to stop visiting pregnancy message boards. I blocked out the internet, turned off the news, and downloaded one of those apps that gives cute week-by-week size correlates ("Your baby is a blueberry!" "Your baby is a troll doll!"). Over the next few weeks, my body grew soft patches of blond fur, and I woke in the middle of the night to scavenge the kitchen for food. Nourished with prenatal vitamins, my nails grew, resembling claws by the time I remembered to trim them. One day, I scratched my chin and clipped what I assumed to be another pimple, only to realize I had crumbs of yesterday's bread caught in my beard. According to my doctor, all of this was normal.

Yet every medical visit seemed to center on potential abnormality. At the nuchal exam, where they measure the baby's neck to screen for Down's syndrome, the technician ran her ultrasound wand through the jelly on my stomach, and there she was, my daughter, in black-and-white film, like a silent movie star. It was the first time we saw her. She sat in my uterus like it was a hammock.

"Looking good," said the technician.

"Does that mean no Down's syndrome?" I asked.

"Chances are now reduced to one in ten thousand," the technician said, and even then I sensed a pattern: now and forever, the best they'd give us would be new versions of still-frightening odds. I watched the blurry skeleton of my daughter wiggle on the screen and squeezed my husband's hand. Our baby stirred less than two feet from my heart, but I couldn't help her. I turned to him and said, "She's all alone in there."

Around that time, I heard P-22 had broken in and out of the Los Angeles Zoo, leaping over an eight-foot wall in one of the enclosures to murder a koala. Later that night, my mouth full of bread and my body a furnace, because it now pumped two hearts, I imagined P-22 surveying the moonlit Hollywood sign, savoring its memories of the delicious flavor of koala bones, waiting for the scent of rodents, or escaped domestic animals, or trespassing teenage potheads—or babies. How could I go into labor in a world where hungry urban pumas were allowed to behave that way?

In the wild, pregnancy makes animals even more vulnerable to predators. But there are strategies for self-defense. I'd read laboratory studies on the effect of predator exposure on pregnant mice; when exposed to rat urine, they refused to give birth. They just gritted their teeth and held it in. If they could do that, so could I. Like an elephant (which gestates for two whole years) I'd simply cross my legs and scream. Eventually P-22 would die, and I'd let the baby fall out.

But my obstetrician said I couldn't refuse to give birth—apparently that's physically impossible. I wasn't a mouse or an elephant, I was a human woman, and I was due on June 2.

The solution was simple: I'd hunt down P-22 and hang his head on the wall of my baby girl's nursery, so that when she became sentient, she would know that her mother was strong and that she was safe.

Getting from point A (finding P-22) to point B (decapitation) remained a mystery to me, but in my blurry state of hormonal unbliss, I simply didn't think about it. Instead, the following day, I laced up my hiking boots, parked my car on the winding road leading to Griffith Park, and set off into the dusty wilderness with only a water bottle, potato chips, and my phone, like a much crazier Cheryl Strayed. She'd gone off trying to find herself. I'd find the lion and take it from there.

He and I had both migrated to Los Angeles. But the city was only big enough for one of us.

* * *

I beeped shut my car door, shoved my water bottle into my biggest coat pocket, and squinted at the sun, feeling hazy. Scholars think pregnancy hormones may enhance protective instincts by enabling women to better recognize fear. Others think it makes us aggressive. In a 1930s article on maternal instinct, scientists found that injecting lady rats with pregnancy hormones brought the females to an undefined "new element of consciousness"—and between the insistent hunger and my absentmindedness, I did feel a little like I'd taken drugs.

But there was nothing eye-opening about my current state. If anything, the fog hanging over Griffith Park mirrored the ecosystem of my brain when I tried to remember

important information, like "When is my due date?" ar
"Where is my nipple Tylenol?" Even then, in my fit of vag
murderous, motherly intention, I really had no idea wh
was prowling around, scoping the trails for mountain li
shit, whatever that looked like. If you had asked me th
what I was doing, I would have peered at you in confusi
like a child. If this was maternal instinct, our species mi
not survive very long.

* * *

In general, eating and walking staved off the persistent nau
so I entered Griffith Park at a fast clip, letting potato cl
dissolve against my tongue as if taking communion, grea
thumbing another round of baby name ideas on my phor
always deleted the lists. Positive outlooks sparked my nat
superstition. God was vengeful, I reasoned, and if the ba
life was really up to chance, too much hopefulness, like a pu
might kill it. To compensate for counting chickens, I glar
at the California sky and did a little apologetic dance for
angels—just a shoulder wiggle with some frowning. I ha
been to church since high school.

I continued on, licking salt off my fingers and rubl
grease off my phone. Pine needles and dead leaves mas
into a red paste underfoot. The trails bumped up against b
yards, and the residents bordering the park had barrica

themselves with chain-link fences and No Trespassing signs. "Too bad cougars can't read," I muttered to myself.

Suddenly, two elderly Asian women plowed past me, wearing sunglasses, sun hats, and sun gloves, poking the dust with hiking poles like a pair of skiing beekeepers and easily overtaking me despite our one-hundred-year age difference. The doctor had said something about my organs moving up, crowding the lungs, mirroring the symptoms of early emphysema. Less than five minutes into the climb, I was completely out of breath. I listened to the steady *thwack* of someone slapping his muddied shoes against a car bumper and thought, "If I turn back now, I can still make the all-day breakfast at that diner near here." But, like a hero, I marched onward.

Halfway up the trail, I stopped to peer inside a corrugated drainage pipe. It seemed like a tight fit for a monster, but how big were mountain lions, anyway? In my efforts to avoid the internet, I hadn't checked. I had, however, seen a three-year-old photograph of P-22 in an old issue of *National Geographic*. In it, he's slinking before the distant, moonlit Hollywood sign, dwarfing the famous white letters.

I switched my attention to the paw prints stamped into the trail. Most were tiny—too small for my culprit—and I wondered at the irresponsibility of that: bringing a Chihuahua, or whatever, to a park where pumas hunted. I stopped

the next dog walker I saw and self-righteously warned him to be careful.

"P-22 just ate a koala," I announced, pointing to his golden retriever for a size comparison.

The guy stared at me. "P-twenty-what?"

I watched them trot away.

Moments later, fighting a sudden urge to pee, I looked around for the dirty park bathrooms but couldn't locate them, and soon found myself racing back to my car, my bladder in emergency mode. "Sorry," I called, hurrying past an unhurried hiker, who was wearing a leopard-print purse as a backpack. Once out of earshot, I turned the apology on my belly button. According to the pregnancy app, she could hear now.

"Sorry," I murmured, skidding down the rest of the rocky slope to my car.

Mommy hadn't killed the monster.

On my way out of the nearest café's bathroom, I called my cousin Jenni, who, like me, was pregnant, but she also had a toddler at home. "All I did today was write about my feelings, take a seven-minute walk, and urinate," I murmured, "and I'm exhausted."

She laughed. "Just wait until you have a screaming baby."

As if on cue, I heard her toddler screech in the background.

Jenni lowered her voice, sounding grave, and added, "Seriously, just wait."

This turned out to be a common refrain. "Just wait" became an obnoxious sound track to my neuroses. Friends who had kids asked how I felt, only to reissue a variation on "If you think that's bad, just wait." Over the next month, I hiked in Griffith Park nearly every day, and even strangers started saying it. "Are you?" they gushed, nodding at my stomach, which stuck out through my hiking clothes—and then: "Any weird symptoms? Cravings? How are you feeling?" I fell for it every time, listing annoying but nondeadly stuff like "I feel pretty stupid," or "I'm hot at night," or "I'm still worried this mountain lion might eat my offspring." And they'd wait for me to finish before issuing the tired punch line: "Just wait"—which seemed to roughly translate to: *If you think that's crazy, you childless innocent, you're in for a true nightmare. Welcome to hell.*

Their veiled warnings reminded me of this one night during my first trimester. Earlier that evening, I'd insisted my husband and I eat chicken liver and spinach for dinner, and afterward he lay on the couch with his head in my lap, digesting, chattering up at me, telling me jokes and being sweet. I don't remember what it was, exactly, only that at one point he said something so funny that I choked on my laughter and barfed all over his face. The liver-colored puke pooled in his eyes and dammed at the corners of his mouth. I scrambled onto the rug to finish puking. My husband peeled off his shirt and used a clean corner to mop my chin and said, "I love you," grimacing at the smell. It marked the first of many moments that now seem specific to pregnancy—a situation in which the surprising ignominy of something totally unexpected gets compounded by knowing things will only get weirder. There we were, covered in my puke, but in eight months, if everything went well, he'd watch my vagina explode.

Then eight months became six, then five, then four and a half—and there I was, a time bomb, counting down to the third trimester. When I rescheduled a session with my psychiatrist so I could, once again, go searching for P-22, my psychiatrist said, "Hmm," and asked whether I might actually be worried about more abstract threats. "Motherhood, sexism, the idea of forever," she offered. "A lot of my female patients are very upset about Trump." She reminded me that at my wedding, the joy my husband and I felt had spasmed when we realized that everyone we loved would probably not be together in the same room again except at our own funerals, and only then if we died young. "For the neurotic, celebrations of life can conjure death," she said. "Pregnancy is a time of regression. It throws the mind into maturational crisis."

I reminded her that sometimes a cigar is just a cigar.

I said, "Anyone who doesn't fear the lion is insane."

*   *   *

The photographer who'd captured that iconic photo of P-22 with the Hollywood sign had called the animal a "ghost cat," and I was starting to understand why; I couldn't find P-22, nor any trace of him. None of the other hikers I spoke with seemed worried—in fact, they rarely knew of his existence. I was starting to feel haunted, like that lady in the horror movie who's trying to warn everyone that death is coming, but they keep saying, "Oh, honey, it's just the wind." After another fruitless hike, I scrawled a long, hysterical list of questions to ask the doctor at my upcoming sonogram—all of them some version of "Is the baby okay?" When I showed it to my husband, he asked me, "Baby, are *you* okay?"

The next day, I was having lunch with my friend Daniela, an otherworldly woman who sometimes texts me about the moon and had once harnessed psychic powers during a dinner party at my place to relay a message from my pet bunny rabbit, Mimosa, in which Mimosa expressed displeasure at my go-to term of endearment: "Fatso Batso." ("Mimosa doesn't like it when you affectionately call her fat," Daniela chided me. "She prefers the term 'beautiful.'") Daniela lives near Griffith Park and has a small child who's koala-sized, so I asked her what she thought of P-22, trying to sound casual.

"Oh, Kathleen, you didn't hear?"

I shook my head, explaining I'd taken a break from the news, and braced myself for some gory tale of dismembered children—the discovery of a mountain lion's nest made out of human bones.

"They scooped him up," Daniela said, reaching for her phone. "Rangers. He ate a diseased rat and got mange." She showed me a side-by-side comparison photo, published on some blog, of P-22 before and after the mange. Prior to getting sick, he'd been photographed in the wild, a resplendent, shiny beast—the same I'd seen in *National Geographic*—muscled and ready for his close-up. Post-mange, he sat in an enclosure, looking grumpy, his features discombobulated. Spiky fur, beady eyes. Even the shape of his head was weird.

"Looks like a bad police sketch," I said.

Daniela nodded. "I have a feeling he was in distress."

She explained that before news broke of the mange, P-22 had appeared to her in a dream.

"I'm under the impression that he understands what pets are and wants to be one," she said, sipping her beet juice. "He said to me, 'Let me live with you,' and I was like, 'What if you eat me?' and he looked at me very gravely and responded, 'I know what food is.'" She cut our vegan samosa with a fork and set aside half for me to eat. "But then he ate the diseased rat."

I poked at my portion of the appetizer, feeling gutted. This whole time I'd been walking around Griffith Park, seeking out a monster that wasn't even there. My psychiatrist had been right. P-22's proximal vitality had given me a false sense of control over my intangible fears. Now he was sickly and pathetic, and the threat of his nearness and whatever fantasy it afforded me had vanished, or at least been contained.

I'm not sure whether the disappointment was evident on my face or whether Daniela's psychic powers were simply kicking in, but she seemed to read my mind.

"Apparently there's another one?" she said, with an optimistic question mark in her voice. "In the Santa Monica Forest—P-41."

My mind raced. Maybe P-41 would cross the freeways, just like P-22, and end up near enough to us that I'd have an excuse for another hunt. But why was I willing him to come closer? That didn't seem motherly. And if the animal did show up, then what? I could hear the chorus of parents: *You think a mountain lion's bad? What about drunk drivers, kidnappers, or the first time she gets her heart broken?* Terrors come in all shapes and sizes. There would always be another puma.

Just wait.

* * *

The next day I went back to Griffith Park and prowled around, idly wondering where P-41 might set up shop. But instead of looking for animal shit, I found myself distracted by the sight of two eight-year-old girls, dancing and singing upbeat songs about puking, their moms in tow, saying, "Pretty melody." Farther up the path, a toddler swung between her parents, shouting, "Look, glitter," her eyes alighting on some silvery garbage poking through the weeds, like she'd just found gold. Her mom glanced at the detritus: a rusty shopping cart stuffed with bulging plastic bags. "Very nice," she said.

I projected us onto that scene, my husband, our daughter, and me. She'd arrive confused and unknowing, wondering who the hell we were, and we would have to show her. I imagined her at three, unencumbered, easily amused, believing rusty, discarded shopping carts were carriages, that trash was pretty treasure. At eight, she'd make up songs about the times she barfed. Just because I was strange and sort of afraid of everything didn't mean I had to scare her. In fact, if she turned out to be anything like me or my husband, she would need some reassuring. We were neurotic, but part of parenting would mean deciding which parts of ourselves to reveal. So we would go to Griffith Park, I decided, during the daylight hours, while lions slept, and point out the nice parts: the dogs and desert flowers and birds, and how bits of garbage underfoot could sparkle in the sunlight, how even in the desert, where the earth crumbled and was dry, life somehow thrived. There would still be pumas, but there would also be us, and we would have one another. It wouldn't always be enough, but it was something: a sense of safety in a predatory world.

Acknowledgments

This book would not be possible without the talent, guidance, and compassion of Betsy Lerner, Peter Blackstock, and Morgan Entrekin. You have my gratitude, admiration, and affection.

In these essays I describe some lonesome moments that might have been intolerable without the incredible support of my closest friends and family: Mom, Dad, Ellie, Drew, Mara, Michael, Carly, Tom, Gail, Michael Hertzberg, Frank, Alex, Nathaniel, Meredith, Jenni, Jemma, Sarah McKetta, Nathan Johnson, Bridget Barry, Amy Heberle, David Iserson, John and Anna Mulaney, Genevieve Angelson, Pinckney Benedict, Jessica Almon Galland, James Gallagher, Mr. and Mrs. Zarwell—and of course, my psychiatrist, Dr. Fox.

I am also deeply indebted to the magazines and websites that first published these essays in their original forms—*Hazlitt* ("Prey"), the *Guardian US* ("Snowflake"), the *Guardian Weekend* ("Catfish"), *Elle* online ("First I Got Pregnant Then I

Decided to Kill the Mountain Lion"), *Mary Review* ("Cricket"), and *Vice* ("I Hunted Feral Hogs as a Favor to the World")—and to all the editors thereof who helped me shape them: Alexandra Molotkow, Jessica Reed, Ruth Spencer, Melissa Denes, Chloe Schama, Mitchell Sunderland, and Jillian Goodman.

As always, I am grateful to my subjects—Susie, Deb, and the people of Snowflake: thank you for opening your lives to me (it is never easy to be written about, I know)—and to those who leant me their time and insight so that I might better understand some of the issues touched on in these essays: Dr. Michael Rich, Nev Schulman, Stephen Dubinsky—and especially Vicki Levi, who provided invaluable research, materials, and priceless advice about the Miss America Pageant, thank you.

Special thanks to filmmaker Mae Ryan and writer Jillian Gagnon, who embarked with me into unknown territory, and generously permitted me to make them characters in my work—and of course to my dear friend Sarah McKetta, who has come with me on more writing assignments than I can count.

Most of all, I am eternally grateful to my husband, Simon, for adoring, encouraging, and inspiring me every day. I love you like crazy. I love you all the time.